The
Jefferson
Hotel

The Jefferson Hotel

The History of a Richmond Landmark

PAUL HERBERT

Charleston | London

THE
History
PRESS

Published by The History Press
Charleston, SC 29403
www.historypress.net

Front cover: "The Jefferson Hotel," by Parks Pegram Duffey III. Used with permission.

Back cover: Courtesy of James Oliver Images.

First published 2012

Manufactured in the United States

ISBN 978.1.60949.687.6

Library of Congress CIP data applied for.

*To Mary Stuart Cruickshank, The Jefferson Hotel historian,
and George T. Ross, the man who saved the hotel from the wrecking ball.*

Contents

CONTENTS

Acknowledgements

G eorge Ross, a prior owner of the hotel, along with his office manager, Ann Dannhausen, must be acknowledged for their assistance and friendship. Going through old documents could never be as enjoyable as doing so while chatting with them.

The family members of some of the other former owners deserve much gratitude for sharing their recollections: Albert Suttle Jr., Grace Suttle, Betsy Watkins Short, Walter Banks and Charles Consolvo III. Mr. Suttle met with me on more than one occasion and provided a photograph of his father.

I appreciate the assistance and support from Bill Shields, Don Pierce, Norma Pierce, John Edmonds, Michael Ajemian, Don James, Cecilia Brooks and Gibson Worsham. Parks Duffey III shared his paintings. Gibson Worsham shared many interesting stories and firsthand recollections about the hotel, and Allen Barringer told me what it was like being a twelve-year-old kid climbing up into the clock towers. The "Stephens Girls"—Marthanne Stephens Smith and Jean Stephens Arrington—shared their recollections. Nancy Jones Albright explained what the hotel was like when she got married there in 1980. Langhorne Gibson moved things along by sharing stories about his grandmother, Irene Langhorne. Mrs. Bettie Terrell Hobson provided great assistance in showing me her scrapbooks about the hotel and about her aunt, Elinor Fry. Campbell David provided her recollections of working on the book *Getty*. And to Susan Powell Williams: thanks for showing me the scrapbooks and making copies for me. Your kindness and enthusiasm are appreciated.

Thanks to the Virginia Historical Society, the Valentine Museum and the Special Collections and Archives, James Branch Cabell Library of the Virginia Commonwealth University (VCU) Libraries. Ray Bonis at VCU deserves special thanks for his kind assistance. The Richmond Public Library shared its clipping file. The Western Historical Manuscript Collection in Rolla, Missouri, provided information about Esther Price, and the Sargeant Memorial Collection of the Norfolk Public Library (special thanks to Robert Hitchings and Troy Valos) gave me stories and photographs related to Charles Consolvo. Heather Moon, Arlene Stewart and Laura Price of the *Richmond Times Dispatch* made the arrangements to let me review the newspaper's clipping file. Ed Jewett at the Marshall Court House allowed me to go through the archives files, and researcher Johnie Clarke researched and copied court filings. I greatly appreciate Sue Dayton and Jim Oliver for letting me use their photos. Hotel executives Rick Butts, Joe Longo and Leta McVeety also assisted in the project.

Finally, thanks to Dabney Denbrock and Mary Stuart Cruickshank. Dabney helped me come up with the idea to write the book and provided encouragement along the way. Mary Stuart, who will forever in my mind be the "hotel historian," spent more time with me working on this project than any other person. I enjoyed all the dinners with Mary Stuart. Who knew that those boxes of old hotel-related documents and photos that she rescued from the dumpster nearly three decades ago would ever be so appreciated?

Prologue

Steeped in history, laden with romance and providing twentieth-century comfort with nineteenth-century ambiance, The Jefferson Hotel is a traveler's dream come true—all travelers, weary or invigorated, old or young. High tea in the lobby—you feel like a character in an old black-and-white movie. Capacious one moment, the lobby mystically transforms into refreshing coziness, the chairs and settees arranged ever so perfectly, with lamps and tables placed with just enough open space. The woman a few yards distant is far away if you want privacy but magically close if you choose to converse. Even in the lobby, you're alone reading your newspaper in the privacy and silence of your own living room. Then, instantly, with a subtle realignment of your eyes over the top of the page, presto, someone comes over and pours more tea or asks if you need anything. Back to the paper, and the invisible walls reappear if that's what you desire. Of all the things worth savoring, my favorite is how the hotel simultaneously balances openness and privacy. Big place, flurry of activity; serene surroundings, quiet relaxation—a uniquely happy blend.

I

The Prettiest Women
and Manly Men

But the Richmond hotel had a marble stair and long unopened rooms
and marble statues of the gods lost somewhere in its echoing cells.
—F. Scott and Zelda Fitzgerald, *"Show Mr. and Mrs. F. to Number --"*

It started with an idea.

Late in the Gilded Age, a grand hotel opened in Richmond, Virginia. For the city, which had been destroyed by the war only three decades earlier, it must have seemed straight out of an H.G. Wells novel. Most Richmonders had never been to a grand hotel. The truth is, outside big northern cities like New York, there weren't many grand hotels. Richmonders bubbled with enthusiasm when the hotel opened on Thursday, October 31, 1895, a day earlier than originally planned, but that original day was a Friday, an ominous day to start anything. The papers gushed with hyperbole and a creative array of artistic superlatives. Much of what Richmonders saw in The Jefferson were things they couldn't have imagined. It had glamour, space—lots of it—and opulence. Lavish and capacious halls and ballrooms, ornate and awe-inspiring, electrically illuminated and furnished and decorated with the most spectacular and expensive accoutrements of the day. Exquisite dining; no expense spared. The walls exuded imagination and vivacity. Everything about it—its richness, its marble—was elegant, stunning and, to many, straight out of fantasy. Residents of Richmond witnessed no civic event that generated as much excitement as the opening of The Jefferson

Hotel. People waited a day in advance just to see it. Visitors the first night, according to the manager, treated the hotel like a church. The *Richmond Dispatch* reported that the hotel

> *seems destined to become one of the great attractions of the entire Southland, and a powerful inducement to the great army of tourists to turn their steps in the direction of this city, so rich in historic associations…Everything connected with the house is on a scale of ultra-magnificence, and, as it now stands, the hostelry is the most complete and luxurious in the South, and takes a place of honor in the foremost rank of representative American hotels.*

Two hundred employees would keep this modern establishment going. Rooms cost $5.00 per night, with a few as low as $3.50. Monthly rentals started at $100.00. It boasted 342 guest rooms (of which 34 were set aside for employees): 85 on the first floor, 79 on the second, 73 on the third, 65 on the fourth, 26 on the fifth and 14 on the mezzanine level. It had the most modern features of the day. Each room was furnished in cypress, and the walls of "King's cement" were painted blue, green, pink, rose or cream.

All rooms had stationary washbowls with running hot and cold water, a trunk rest (so guests wouldn't hurt their backs) and a mantel adorned with beveled mirrors. Some of the rooms had fireplaces; others, steam radiators. Several rooms had private bathrooms with handsome porcelain bathtubs. Each floor had a women's bathroom at one end and a men's at the other. The first hotel in America with a bathroom for every bedroom was the Mount Vernon Hotel in the resort town of Cape May, New Jersey, in 1853. It took about a half century before other hotels offered such extravagance.

Each room boasted the brand-new Herzog Teleseme (spelled various ways, including Tellesame), a device patented the same year the hotel opened. The word comes from "tele" as in telephone and "seme" as in semaphore. Its means: "to signal from afar." It allowed guests to turn an indicator control in their room to select the service they needed. The dials had various settings, such as waiter, maid and valet, and were operated by electricity. The communication was faster and more direct than buzzing the front desk and waiting for someone to come up and ask what you wanted. As for the telephone, The Jefferson Hotel's phone number at the beginning was Madison 6680.

The electric lights were something to behold, a fact remarked upon by many, which is not surprising when you consider electric lights had been introduced to many Americans just two years earlier at the World's Exposition. Local girl Helena Lefroy Caperton, who had been used to gas lighting, recalled that the electric lights appeared as "a revelation…the shaded brilliance like fairyland." Even the water fountains were illuminated at night with electric lights. The hotel had luxurious Roman, Turkish, electric and hydro-therapeutic baths, the magical elixir to good health, as well as roof gardens where performers entertained under the stars. The hallway wires were out of view, encased in brass tubes. Everything you could want, and nothing was overlooked. It had a writing room, a barbershop, news and cigar booths and a drugstore. The bar boasted a thousand-bottle wine closet, and the library was well stocked with books. A ladies' billiard room on the fifth floor overlooked Jefferson Street. Nearby on the fifth floor were rooms for germans (dances), meetings and a place to keep refreshments to supply the roof gardens.

The Palm Court, where real alligators resided for five decades. *Courtesy of James Oliver Images.*

The Palm Court had real grass and even real alligators. A creative genius like Lewis Ginter was going to make sure the Palm Court earned its name. In stories a few days before the hotel opened, the *Richmond Dispatch* referred to the upper lobby area as the Arcade, and the *Richmond Times* called it the Franklin Street court or the Winter Garden. According to the *Times*:

> *From the north and south sides around the statue, and extending to the walkway of the corridor, are two basins of marble, highly decorated, with a dozen or more miniature fountains, sending forth from either side their sparkling spray, in such a manner as to form perfect arches. These produce a brilliant effect with the electric lights bringing out their beauty. Each basin is bordered by a natural evergreen growth, two feet in height. Between the basins…there are spreading palms, bay trees, cactuses, and tropical plants of various kinds, shipped from the West Indies and South America.*

The Thomas Jefferson Statue originally faced north toward Franklin Street. In the Ladies' Café, off the Palm Court, "the rapidly developing ambition of the modern woman to enjoy 'man's' privileges found a favored spot." One room was called the Pink Parlor; another—with a $1,000 Steinway grand piano—the Green Parlor.

Even the paintings adorning the walls were world class. One of them was *Les Bulles de Savon*, or *The Soap Bubbles*. Done in 1890 by Elizabeth Jane Gardner Bouquereau, the sixty-four- by forty-six-inch masterpiece was exhibited at the 1893 Chicago World Exposition. It is believed Ginter purchased it after seeing it at the exposition.

Next to the registration desk hung a gigantic bell, previously used as a timekeeper for the workers during construction. The bell stayed after construction was finished and was used as a good-luck token. Opening-night dinner included Bluepoint oysters, broiled striped bass with lobster sauce, leg of mutton, chicken sauté, venison and fillet mignon.

One early publication referred to the new hotel as the "Aristocrat of Southern Hotels" and provided this commentary:

> *Appreciation of the classics is expressed in the decoration and architecture. The walls of the grand salon, the reception rooms and the library are hung with meritorious paintings and their windows and doorways with luxurious draperies—rooms rich with thick carpets and beautiful*

Above: *Les Bulles de Savon*, or *The Soap Bubbles*. Exhibited at the 1893 World's Fair. *Courtesy of James Oliver Images*.

Left: Close-up of *The Soap Bubbles*. *Courtesy of Mary Stuart Cruickshank*.

*brocades. The blended colors present an effect of perfect harmony…
Through the huge glass dome of one of the two spacious courts, the
natural light falls on a noble statue of Thomas Jefferson standing
in easy poise. About the court runs a wide arcade supported by great
Corinthian columns. Opening to its marble walls, banked by refreshing
palms and hedges, are the ladies' café and the writing rooms…there is
no crowding or skimping of space. It is…said to have the largest lobby
of any hotel in the world.*

The *Richmond Dispatch* opined, "Everything connected with the house
is on scale of ultra-magnificence, and, as it now stands, the hostelry
is the most complete and luxurious in the South, and takes a place
of honor in the foremost rank of representative American hotels." It
was said to be one of the finest hotels in the world. "The courts, with
fountains, flowers, turf, and electric-lights, are like scenes from the
Arabian Nights. A fine orchestra furnishes good music every night…
Saturday nights the lobbies are crowded with the prettiest and best
dressed women and manly men."

Helena Lefroy Caperton wrote many delightful short stories dealing
with her hometown. One is about working as a hostess at The Jefferson.
In "Welcome," she describes the hotel: "Covering half a city block, it
stands suave and stately, a perfect bit of Spanish architecture…It is a
fitting gateway between the North and South…[Many guests from the
North] regard this hotel as an oasis in a desert…the only civilized spot
between the Pennsylvania Station [in New York City] and Palm Beach!"

Women had what was generally referred to as the women's
entrance on Franklin Street. But anyone could enter or exit the hotel
from whatever side they wanted. The women's entrance was really
the "family-friendly" entrance, shielding children and women from
traveling salesmen. In addition, carriages could drive into the hotel to
unload baggage at the Jefferson Street entrance. The men's entrance on
Main Street is where you'd find the rougher set, with men occasionally
swearing and spitting.

Guests entering the Rotunda from Main Street were greeted by a
collection of features dedicated to men: a barbershop, a bar, a railroad
ticket office, a telegraph office and a fifty-square-foot smokers' hall, "a
veritable El Dorado to all lovers of the fragrant weed." On the east side
of the Rotunda, holding six Monarch billiards and pool tables, stood
a billiards room furnished in light oak. The original registration area

was on the Rotunda level, to the left as you entered from Main Street, where TJ's Restaurant is located today. The registration desk wasn't moved to its current location upstairs until 1986. There's an area on the floor right outside TJ's where you can feel how the weight of all those travelers through the years wore down the tiles.

Any aspect of the hotel might have been the most dazzling, but for many it was the architecture. *Interior Design* magazine mentioned this about the hotel's architecture: "Pompeian, Louis XVI, Victorian, Colonial Renaissance—all of it and more can be found." Brad Elias, who worked with Carole Hochheiser in designing the hotel in the mid-1980s, opined, "They just threw in everything. It's wacky and wonderful, but it looks charming and it works." Edwin Slipek Jr. wrote in *Style Weekly*, "If architecture is theatre, The Jefferson interior is like a movie set: Those passing through feel like Garbo. And the level changes magnify the drama."

Forty-three guests registered the first day, the first being John H. Fowler of Baltimore. It took several years of planning to get to that first day. Perhaps the earliest identifiable day in the hotel's history was sometime in 1881, when the newspaper reported local leaders were discussing the need for a prominent hotel in Richmond. The president of the Richmond Chamber of Commerce stated in his annual report, "Thousands pass through the city yearly who would be glad to stop over if they could be assured of such accommodations as are offered in towns of half our population in eastern states." Three years later—by March 1884—fourteen citizens and/or entities promised to donate a total of $103,000 toward a new hotel. Peter H. Mayo, James H. Dooley and Joseph Bryan, three men who would later someday own The Jefferson Hotel, agreed to $5,000 each. Lewis Ginter subscribed for $10,000. The Jefferson was just a distant mirage, more than a decade away, but they were on the journey to get there.

In January 1893, it was reported, plans to build The Jefferson had been extended a month from the original deadline to February 1. Messrs. Poindexter and Bryant of Richmond presented a drawing, as did New York architects Carrere and Hastings. Other architectural drawings were expected from Baltimore, Philadelphia and Atlanta. On February 21, 1893, the *Dispatch* reported: "The first step towards building The Jefferson Hotel...was taken yesterday when the work of tearing down the brick walls which enclose the site of the great hostelry were taken down. The fact that the new hotel has become a certainty was hailed with delight."

the "Plunge Room," its three-thousand-gallon tub freshened with five hundred gallons of clean water poured in each hour. Finally, it was on to a massage. A promotional piece touted the baths' "superior medical attendants [who were] provided with all the necessary apparatus and appliances for giving practical and scientific treatment. These baths are especially remedial in cases of gout, rheumatism, chlorosis [sic], anemia, hysteria, especially hysterical spine, hysterical paralysis, neurasthenia, neuralgias, especially sciatica, etc."

At the start, Thomas Rimmer handled the men's operations, which ran from 2:00 p.m. to 10:00 p.m. His wife and her crew took care of ladies' hours, from 9:00 a.m. to 2:00 p.m. Later managers included Professor Victor Schrwald of St. Petersburg and Professor Wolverton from New York. The hotel kept daily reports of all facets of operations. The report for October 20, 1899, revealed that the eleven Turkish baths that day earned the operators eight dollars.

The grand hotel got off to an exciting start. A month after it opened, the American Association of Educators and Writers met to discuss the Civil War's Wilderness Campaign. Other groups meeting at the hotel included the National Society of the Sons of the American Revolution, the United Confederate Veterans and the Merchants Tailors' National Exchange. The tailors were welcomed by Mayor Taylor. At their banquet, the members were "enriched by all the delicacies for which the Old Dominion is far famed." Later, the delegates enjoyed an oyster roast at Lakeside and "were driven about the city." According to one story, "To sum up the whole matter, the Richmond folks were simply lavish in their hospitality."

The National Education Association convened at what the *Trenton* [New Jersey] *Evening Times* called the "famous Jefferson Hotel, the finest place in the South." In November 1899, the United Daughters of the Confederacy held its sixth annual convention in the roof gardens. At the meeting, Mrs. James Leigh presented a gavel made by a Confederate soldier from a tree under which General Lee made his last speech to his soldiers.

The American Bankers Association had its twenty-sixth annual convention in October 1900. Its 4,500 members had combined deposits exceeding $5.1 billion, and those figures did not include the capital and deposits of the 432 members who were private bankers. As part of the convention, the attendees went to a local church to hear eighty-six-year-old Reverend John Jaspers preach his famous "Sun Do

Move" sermon, in which he "delivered his views of the solar system with all his old-time vigor. The bankers were highly entertained."

John Jaspers, born on the Fourth of July 1812 and formerly a slave, preached for many years to enormous crowds "in a torrent of language that has never been equaled." Between 1878 and 1901, Jaspers preached his hour-and-a-half sermon, according to one source, more than 250 times, "painting word-pictures with such mastery that he had people alternately shouting in elation and crying in anguish. It was oratorical eloquence at its finest." Using biblical references, Jaspers asserted that the earth was flat and the sun moved around the earth. According to one biographer, Jaspers was a "national character, and he and his philosophy were known from one end of the land to the other."

In June 1900, the Seaboard Air Line Railway hosted a banquet for four hundred to celebrate the opening of a direct line between Baltimore and Tampa. The *Baltimore American* reported that guests arrived in Richmond "amid booming of cannon, blasts of whistle and waving of handkerchiefs from windows and balconies." Upon completion at Richmond's Main Street station, three-year-old John Skelton Williams Jr. hammered in the golden spike for the new railway. He ended up getting to keep it because his father, Seaboard president John L. Williams, bought it at auction for $250. Williams was quoted as saying that the new Seaboard was not the result of one man or even a group of men but rather of the people of the South. He boasted that the railway system was owned entirely by southerners, and "not one cent [was] owed to a financial institution north of Baltimore."

At the party, several toasts were made. Governor J. Hoge Tyler toasted the state of Virginia, and John Williams drank to the Seaboard. Other toasts included the Cities on the Seaboard, Cities to Be on the Seaboard, the Island of Cuba and the Open-Door Policy. One thing the guests probably got a good look at were the reptilian creatures up in the Palm Court.

ALLIGATORS

You might think live alligators crawling around a hotel in Richmond would have been reported and written about frequently or at least occasionally. But they were very rarely mentioned. Hotel guests who wrote letters and postcards to loved ones often described the hotel but didn't mention the alligators. When Harry Truman wrote home to his wife in 1940, he told her what a great hotel The Jefferson was, and even described it, but didn't say a word about alligators. But that seems to have been the norm. The alligators were there, and people saw them, but hardly anyone seems to have written about them. Look at the newspaper stories when the hotel opened in 1895 and when it reopened in 1907—long, detailed stories—and you won't find a word about alligators, something you might expect if alligators were a common feature of the area or if all hotels had alligators. But there was nothing common about The Jefferson having alligators. It's incredible, even a little maddening, that no one seemed to notice the alligators or bother writing about them. To me, this conspicuous omission was the single oddest thing about the history of the hotel. I can't explain it and can't even come up with a workable theory. This lack of reportage is exactly why there is some confusion today about the alligators. It proved a real challenge to get the dots connected to form a complete, accurate picture.

Many people know or have heard the stories about how the "snow birds" from Richmond and cities farther north brought alligators back in the spring on their way home after a winter in Florida. True. A man named Allen Tunis wrote to the hotel years ago to report that his father gave the hotel, in 1927, two alligators named Mutt and Jeff. The Tunis family later moved to New York and didn't make it back to the hotel until 1934. Alligators were still in the Palm Court, but the Tunises couldn't tell if they were Mutt and Jeff.

Anne Poyner Walker reported that when she was a little girl, her grandmother sent her an alligator from Florida. She kept it in her bathtub for a while but eventually gave it to The Jefferson. Martha Cronley, the hotel's social secretary during the Depression, recalled that the alligators were given to children at Christmas as pets and subsequently "wore out their welcome." Maude Martin of Bracey, Virginia, recalled going over to The Jefferson to see the alligators. Anne Ivey stated that her brother brought an alligator—named Sugo—back from Florida. Shortly afterward, they realized they needed their bathtub more than they needed the alligator, so Sugo went off to The Jefferson. Doug Wherry of Chesterfield kept his alligators at The Jefferson when he wintered in Florida; when he returned to Virginia, he brought them back home with him.

James Cheatham, a Jefferson employee in the 1920s, recalled that there were two alligator ponds—one for Pompey and the other for the smaller alligators, often as many as eight or nine. Bettie Terrell Hobson stated that her mother threatened to feed her to the alligators if she didn't finish her dinner. Jane Young shared an anecdote in family lore involving her father, "Bunt" Ragland. Sometime around 1910, when Bunt was about fifteen years old, he and a buddy, being young boys looking for something original and fun to do, tied strings or ropes around two alligators and took them strolling down Franklin Street one summer afternoon. The boys were promptly whisked away to the police station. After conferring over the telephone with Bunt's father, the judge gave the boys a good talking to and made them walk home.

One woman who was born across the street from the hotel in 1905 recalled seeing

> there, in a white pool, a huge alligator lay dormant. He looked evil when he was asleep, and even more so when he opened one eye and winked. There were three smaller alligators in the pool, and they showed a little vitality, but not the old one. A friend whose family had brought a baby alligator back with them from Florida eventually gave it to the hotel after they got tired of it. The old alligator gobbled it up in one bite, right before their eyes.

In his autobiography, *The Moon's a Balloon*, actor David Niven wrote about the alligators: "My eyes gummed together with tiredness snapped open with amazement when, just as I was signing the hotel register, I noticed a full-sized alligator in a pool about six feet from the reception desk." Niven was a little mixed up about where he saw them, as the registration desk was downstairs in the Rotunda and the alligator pools (otherwise known as rills) were located up in the Palm Court, on either side of the Thomas Jefferson Statue.

A longtime hotel doorman reported, "Every night Pompey would crawl out of the pond and sleep in a chair, right here in the lobby." Thomas Herbert of the Rotunda Club stated, "They used to get out from time to time, and we'd find them all over the hotel." Guests sometimes complained that the alligators' "anguished wails" kept them awake. Jefferson employee Edward Ellis claimed that Pompey, eight to nine feet in length, made sounds "like a cow mooing," which brought some hotel employees running with brooms and mops. Pompey clamped down on the bristled end, and an employee gently pulled or tugged him back to his pool. When another alligator died at the hotel, the *Richmond News Leader* had these thoughtful words: "For twenty years—from the days of his 'gator babyhood—Mike lived in the shallow pool beneath the potted palms…There he spent his waking hours gazing at the famous statue of Thomas Jefferson, or blinking with sleepy boredom…Mike was indifferent to art, to celebrities and to all the sightseers who gazed at him."

Oscar West, a porter who retired in 1964 after working at The Jefferson for fifty years, recalled when Pete, the meanest and largest of all the alligators, crawled into the reading room and scared a near-sighted lady who had mistaken him for a footrest. He also recalled Pompey swallowing a diamondback terrapin that was supposed to be someone's dinner. West said the hotel first tried feeding them steak, but they didn't like it. Goldfish worked because alligators ate "anything that was alive." The *Times Dispatch* reported in October 1964 that back in 1936, a retired army colonel fell into the alligator pool, requiring nine stitches.

A review of Richmond newspapers reveals alligators were very much in the news at the time the hotel was built. In April 1893, the "Richmond elite" attended a bazaar where an alligator was auctioned. Perhaps this was the time, as construction of The Jefferson was starting, that Mr. Ginter thought to put live alligators in the Palm Court. A month before The Jefferson Hotel opened, the *Richmond Times* reported that a twenty-three-inch alligator had been caught near Fredericksburg, Virginia. Richmond newspapers at the time carried stories about the financial benefits of alligator farms and about how alligators at the New York Zoo were so content as to be almost harmless. The papers reported several incidents of people finding alligators in their kitchens, their yards or nearby streams in and around Richmond. In 1902, a Leigh Street resident offered to trade his seven-foot alligator—which he had had stuffed—for something of equal value. One man found an alligator near his house in May 1900. The story mentioned that the creature might have escaped from Lakeside Park, "where several were kept last year." A resident near the capitol in Richmond claimed one of his alligators was lost for two weeks until it reappeared in his yard. In July 1904, George Valentine auctioned tools, furniture and a live alligator, listed in the advertisement as a pet. The Nature Study Department in Farmville, Virginia, received a gift of two alligators in 1903 from a man who brought them back from Florida. Virginia soldiers stationed in Florida during the Spanish-American War in 1898 promised to send or bring alligators back to Richmond.

The main questions were when did the alligators first show up at the hotel, why did they show up and when did they leave? Getting those answered requires untangling a lot of information and accounts, much of them incomplete and conflicting. The alligators are a storied part of the hotel's history and a great tradition that lasted about half a century. The hotel's iconic figure is the alligator, and rightfully so. This reptilian creature taking up residence in a grand hotel like The Jefferson was remarkable.

Several people over the years have claimed that the alligator tradition started when the hotel reopened in 1907. I reviewed the newspaper stories of the era but saw no mention of this. I read the letters Joseph Bryan wrote at the time the hotel reopened in 1907. There's a wide array of topics mentioned, but nothing about alligators.

When the alligators first appeared is directly connected to *why* they appeared. Lewis Ginter had a reason to have alligators when he opened the hotel in 1895. Think Palm Court. Imagine you are going to open a hotel and money is no issue whatsoever. His only concern was doing things on a grand scale. Whatever his imagination could conjure, he could and would do. One thing about Lewis Ginter, besides his money and love of Richmond, was that he was, as mentioned earlier, incredibly imaginative. If you had a room called the Palm Court, with real grass and palm trees and exotic plants brought in from the West Indies and South America, what creature would be a natural accruement to the setting? Alligators! Of course it started in 1895 because Lewis Ginter, the man with the brilliant and creative mind, wouldn't have an area called the Palm Court without alligators! If he had a room to replicate a South American farm, he would have brought in llamas. If he had set up a deep-sea area, rest assured there would have been a huge shark aquarium.

Additional proof that the alligators were there at the beginning comes in a letter to the editor of *Commonwealth* magazine in March 1951 from Lewis C. Williams. In his firsthand description of rescuing the Jefferson Statue during the fire of 1901, Williams claimed the statue was tipped over onto a mattress, and the head broke off when they dragged it over the alligator bath: "At this point the [ceiling] glass began to fall, and in our haste to pull the mattress into one of the alcoves, we rolled Mr. Jefferson's statue out of bed and into the alligator's bath, breaking its neck." Certainly, Lewis Ginter would not have gone to the trouble of installing alligator baths and then leave the alligators out.

But the final proof that the alligators started in 1895, when the doors first opened, rests in a firsthand description of someone who was there. Our keeper of the hotel's history, Helena Lefroy Caperton, walked through the hotel with the other guests and visitors on opening night. In an essay published in 1949, she mentioned her surprise in seeing live alligators that night. Years may play tricks on memory, but a seventeen-year-old girl seeing live alligators is not going to get confused about that. The minute she saw them in the hotel, the memory was indelibly etched into her consciousness:

> *The Jefferson Hotel was opened to the public on October 31st, 1895, but before hand there was a gathering of Major Lewis Ginter's personal friends, and to my breathless delight I received an invitation. Dressed in my best "party dress" I followed my elders and betters through those enchanted halls. In these extravagant days, we take luxury and beauty for granted, and our hostelries vie with one another in rococo costliness, but in its pristine freshness The Jefferson was really beautiful…In those rather sparse days of Victorian influence, it all astounded us with its lavish beauty…The discovery of the alligators in the marble tanks of the Palm Court was an added ecstasy. At that youthful and barbaric condition of personal taste I admired them beyond words.*

When did the alligator tradition stop, and what happened to the last alligators? In September 1936, it was reported that alligators Oscar and Pompey died at the New Jefferson Hotel in Richmond, Virginia. (The hotel was often still called "new" from the 1907 rebuilding.) Oscar was believed to have choked from eating a turtle and Pompey from either old age or paint fumes from a remodeling of the lobby. Years later, two longtime hotel employees, John Eggleston and Daniel Mann, said Pompey died the night the alligator pool exploded. They didn't know what caused the pool to explode but speculated that it might have been from ammonia in the water. But there were alligators after that for a few more years. Somewhere in the mix, date unknown, an alligator named Mike died. A Richmond paper ran a story on April 15, 1948, reporting that the last hotel alligator died of old age. Hotel manager A. Gerald Bush was quoted as saying he didn't know how long it had been around, but it had been there for as long as he had, which was about fifteen years. They seemed to die off all at once, no one knows why. One newspaper speculated that someone killed them. Oscar West believed fumes from the Rotunda Club paint job might have done them in, an impossibility since the discussion to start the Rotunda Club didn't even begin until the fall of 1949, a year after the last alligator died. The alligator rills in the Palm Court were removed in about 1950 during one of the early renovations of the Rotunda Club. A story from 1955 stated, "The lethargic alligators, long since called to a happier hunting ground, had been the subject of controversy for some time—a Florida jungle symbol hardly in keeping with the Old Dominion's heights of Monticello or, for that matter, midtown Richmond."

It appears the hotel temporarily stopped the alligator tradition after the 1901 fire and then brought them back again after reopening in 1907. One Richmond paper wrote on April 2, 1905, "Among other good things the gentle spring will bring will be a little rest for the Florida alligators, rest from the prodding of the northern tourists." So by 1905, the subject of bringing alligators back north was already a common enough occurrence that this writer mentioned it. And remember, the hotel did not fully reopen until two years later—in 1907. The reason the alligators would get "rest from the prodding of the northern tourists"? Because The Jefferson was running at half operation and probably got rid of the alligators during this period. From 1901 to 1907, there was no hotel in Richmond where one could drop off the alligators, so people left them in Florida during this period.

There were later attempts to bring them back in some form or another. A *Times Dispatch* story of October 4, 1964, reported that management was planning to bring the alligators back. That same month, the Lambda Chi fraternity of the University of Richmond donated two fourteen-inch alligators to The Jefferson. They were kept in tanks on the Rotunda level, in an aquarium on the registration desk, in the northeast corner of the room or in the northwest corner near the elevator, depending on who's telling the story. The alligators may have been there for as many as four years, as people have adamantly told me they vividly recall the alligators still being there in 1968. But like many things, it's not clear. Others who were at the hotel in 1968 definitely say there were no alligators at that time, and if there had been, they certainly would have known. From everything I've heard, read and seen, I don't think they were there in 1968 (or any time after 1948), with the exception of a few short, temporary displays. They were a source of excitement and wonder to hundreds of thousands of residents and tourists. Many Richmond-area residents still fondly recall the thrill of going to the hotel to see the alligators.

In March 1975, the hotel put three small newts (small salamanders) in a tank in the northeast corner of the Rotunda. A local thirteen-year-old kid had written to the newspaper offering to donate them to the hotel, and manager William Hood took him up on it. The kid agreed to change the water every two weeks, and the hotel fed the creatures. At the same time, a potential buyer for the hotel named Joseph Stettinius playfully called his investment group the Alligator Corporation and said he'd bring the alligators back if he acquired the hotel. The group that bought the hotel in 1983 tried to bring the alligators back but couldn't get approval to do so. They settled for building alligator rills again, in the same place where they were originally located, and filled them in with plants and ersatz alligators. They also put faux alligators in a pond outside, but a bunch of guys from a wedding party ended up stomping on them and cracking them to pieces. They were never put back in the pond after that. In May 1985, the new hotel owners raffled an "elegant, genuine alligator skin" attaché case valued at $1,500. The promotional material mentioned, "Even the alligators that roamed the hotel will be here—albeit in a sculptured state." The alligators you see today in the hotel were sculpted by Paul Jeffries of New York. He created them from joined sheets of hardened lead pressed together. They were hand-shaped; no casts were used.

Ringling Bros. and Barnum & Bailey Circus brought a live alligator to The Jefferson Palm Court lobby for a press conference in February 1988. When the hotel "reopened" in November 1991 under new management, it brought in about a half dozen baby alligators and one of about three to four feet long. In the late 1980s, the hotel had a restaurant on the Franklin Street patio called Old Pompey's Place, the menu showing a drawing of an alligator sitting at a table, legs crossed and drink in hand.

ENTERTAINMENT

Mrs. Herbert A. Claiborne hosted a library party and tea in November 1900 with "some of the loveliest society girls in the city." Each table represented a different book, the name of which was to be guessed by the audience. The person guessing the most books won a prize. Captain Harrie Webster, U.S. Navy, held a five-part lecture series in February and March 1901. Sponsored by the Richmond Arts Club, and costing twenty-five cents' admission, the lectures included "lantern slides" from negatives taken by Webster. The topics were Hawaii, Samoa, Korea, China and Japan. For other international meetings, P.A.S. Brine, British vice-consul, requested "all who sympathize with Great Britain in the present war" (the Boer War) to meet at The Jefferson on January 30, 1900, to establish a South African patriotic fund.

The hotel's first wedding may have been on October 29, 1896, when a man named Walker married a woman named Walker. Frank Walker, thirty-one, of England married Sarah Phoebe Walker, twenty-one, of San Francisco, "a charming and pretty woman." The *Dispatch* wrote, "Around the marriage there is just a tinge of the romantic." Captain Walker commanded a steamer with cargo consigned to Richmond merchants. The bride and her mother traveled across the continent and arrived several days before the wedding, staying in a Jefferson bridal suite. The vows were pledged, "which made Miss Walker Mrs. Walker." The couple remained in Richmond for a day or two before "embarking on their voyage through life on [Captain Walker's] ship." Approximately 110 years later, their grandson Donald Walker mailed to the hotel a copy of the marriage certificate. In October 1900, the hotel hosted two dinners to celebrate two upcoming weddings: Sadie May Thalhimer to Alfred S. Koch of Philadelphia and Hattie Virginia Sycle to Edward Eigenbrun of Petersburg. Both parties took place in the roof gardens.

THE ROOF GARDEN[1]

Another awe-inspiring allurement of the new hotel were the two roof gardens. The Franklin Street–side roof garden (the smaller of the two) was described as "one handsome feature" by *Harper's Weekly* in December 1895. The *Dispatch* reported that it was "equally as pretty" as the other, larger roof garden, which was 140 by 46 feet and seated 1,142. Shortly afterward, for the price of $1,000, an architect named

---

1. Much of the information about the Langhorne-Gibson wedding comes from *Style Weekly* stories by Edwin Slipek Jr.

Edgerton Rogers submitted plans to convert the roof garden on the Main Street side into a winter theater, with movable glass to be taken away in summer. On June 29, 1896, a European-style rooftop theater opened. Several guest rooms were converted to dressing rooms. A promotional description announced, "It is lighted at night by incandescent lamps, attached to the arches that span the garden. It is decorated with trailing vines and palms. The floor of the garden is of slate blocks about 12 inches square. The garden is surrounded by terra-cotta balustrade…At the east end of the garden is erected a stage 26 feet wide and 20 feet deep. The proscenium arch is decorated after the style of Louis XIV."

Early on, Richmonders could see a five-act show on the garden— reserved seats were fifty cents; general admission, a quarter. Performers included a female impersonator who called himself the "Male Maw" and an eccentric song-and-dance artist named Tom Peasley, famous for manipulating his body in unusual ways. The vaudeville shows were so popular that they were extended eleven weeks. But the high prices killed the garden; other Richmond-area outdoor theaters offered vaudeville acts for half the price. By 1898, management was looking to lease out the operation. They had a couple bidders and in June 1898 rented it out to Messrs. Crew and McLaughlin of the Forest-Hill Electric Park for the summer months. The Forest Hill owners didn't have much financial success either. In 1899, the Bijou Family Theatre opened as Richmond's first indoor vaudeville house. The Bijou owner, Jake Wells, later took control of The Jefferson Roof Gardens. But Wells couldn't make a go of it, either. A story in the *Dispatch* two days after the 1901 fire reported, "Many national bodies were scheduled to hold their annual meetings in The Jefferson Roof Garden." The roof gardens were not rebuilt or reopened after the 1901 fire.

It's not known if the Jarretts ever performed at the hotel's roof garden. But the group, which billed itself as "Royal Marionettes—Talking, Singing, Dancing Figures, Pantomime, Comic Opera, Tragedy and Drama," had sent a letter asking to be booked in July 1898 for sixty dollars for a two-week gig.

The wedding of the era in Richmond took place on Thursday, November 7, 1895, when Irene Langhorne, the consummate Richmond belle, married the famous New York artist Charles Dana Gibson at St. Paul's Episcopal Church. Sinclair Lewis called Irene the "Helen of Troy and Cleopatra of her day." The couple had met at a New York horseshow. One newspaper reported that Gibson earned about $25,000 per year for his brilliant drawings—primarily of women—later to be popularly known as the Gibson Girls. Gibson sold his drawings to many publications, including *Scribner's*, *Life*, *Collier's* and *Harper's*.

Many guests coming into town for the wedding stayed at The Jefferson. One of the ushers was Thomas Hastings of Carrere and Hastings. Also at the wedding were Lewis Ginter, John Pope, Grace Arents, Miss Helena Lefroy, Governor and Mrs. O'Ferrall, Sally May Dooley (wife of Major James Dooley), architect Stanford White (who had designed New York City's Madison Square Garden), Nicholas Longworth of Cincinnati (who, along with about sixty other suitors, had earlier proposed to Irene Langhorne), Ethel Barrymore and a woman named Miss Pemberton, who had just injured her ankle while dancing at a Jefferson Roof Garden party. In his book *The Gibson Girl: Portrait of a Southern Belle*, Langhorne Gibson Jr. (Irene's grandson) included a quotation attributed to Dick Davis, one of Gibson's friends. Davis called The Jefferson "a bully hotel as big as the Waldorf with prices in keeping." Davis's party of twenty-five stayed at The Jefferson, "where elegant apartments had been engaged for them."

Following the wedding, the Langhornes hosted a luncheon at their home, 101 West Grace Street (southwest corner of Grace and Adams), catered by The Jefferson Hotel. Among other delights, the guests were treated to iced grapefruit flavored with sherry, panned oysters, boned turkey with truffles, quail, chicken salad, Rhine wine and champagne. After the luncheon, the newlyweds headed for the Hygeia Hotel in Old Point Comfort before starting their yearlong round-the-world honeymoon. From their home on Manhattan's Upper East Side, Irene made many trips back to Richmond. In March 1927, *Time* magazine did a cover story about Charles Dana Gibson, and in 1942, *Life* magazine called the Gibsons "America's most romantic couple."

In November 1900, a woman's shoe, mysteriously wrapped in a pink bow and shipped in rice, was delivered to the hotel. It turns out a couple had just been married in New York, and apparently one of their friends mailed the shoe after the ceremony. The newlyweds were headed to The Jefferson but hadn't yet arrived.

To get an idea of prices of the day, a menu from May 1900 shows that a large porterhouse steak with mushrooms—for the princely sum of $2.50—was the most expensive selection. At $0.05, a glass of buttermilk was the least expensive. Lobster Newburg cost $1.00; a bowl

"Matrimonial Misfits." Drawing by Charles Dana Gibson. *Courtesy of The Jefferson Hotel.*

of green turtle soup was $0.50; turkey with cranberry sauce, $0.60; sirloin steak, $0.80; pork chops, $0.40; a ham and cheese sandwich, $0.25; a slice of apple pie, $0.10; stuffed squab, $0.50; stewed oysters $0.35; and for breakfast, an omelette [*sic*] with rum was $0.50 and scrambled eggs with bacon, $0.40. There were ten different ways you could have your potatoes: boiled, mashed, French fried, Saratoga, stewed in cream, round fried, julienned, hashed brown, Lyonnaise and sautéed.

A newspaper advertisement from January 1900 boasted that The Jefferson Hotel used Pillsbury's best flour, oat flakes and vitos [*sic*]. In July 1898, the hotel announced that during the summer months it would serve individual breakfast and dinner menus for businessmen: "Quickly served and at moderate prices." The price for a hotel room as of January 1900 was two dollars and upward. If you just wanted a newspaper, Billy Mickens was the kid to see. The *Dispatch* wrote in August 1898 about the eight-year-old boy who delivered papers every day and liked to stop at his "hanging-out place," The Jefferson: "His little legs, brown with exposure to sun and begrimed with the dirt of the streets are flying always like the spokes of an old-fashioned spinning wheel." Billy the Newsboy made about five to ten cents a day.

CRIME AND ACCIDENTS

Certainly, The Jefferson had its share of crime and accidents. Perhaps the first casualty in the hotel's history was a moulder named William Armstrong. On March 8, 1894, Armstrong had approached Mr. Sterling, the foreman, about getting work at the hotel. Armstrong, clearly under the influence of liquor, became incensed and used abusive language. Upon being refused, he forced his way into the construction area and ended up dead a few minutes later after falling or jumping thirty feet from the second floor. On September 1, 1897, two workers—Robert Robertson and Prince Carter—were crushed to death at The Jefferson when a twenty-foot pit caved in. The pit was in the alley, just east of the hotel.

A con against the hotel in February 1900 involved a crook named Frank Slayton, "a rather handsome dressy man of good family connections." A career criminal by the age of twenty-five, he had tried years earlier to pass himself off as Robert E. Lee Jr. He had just been released from Eastern State Hospital in Williamsburg, Virginia. Instead of going to jail, he got committed as insane. The *Times* reported that he was "committed for moral insanity but better explained as family influence…he is highly connected." While at Eastern State, he "dressed nicely, played tennis and croquet and enjoyed himself generally, having the freedom of the town…He is a slick talker and his insanity is no worse than that of many another less highly connected boy who has made his living by forgery, robbery and the balance of the category of crime." Slayton, who stayed for about ten days at The Jefferson, was indicted for passing a phony fifty-dollar check. Coincidentally, a couple named Mr. and Mrs. Frank Slayton Thompson were performing a recital at The Jefferson Hotel at this same time—in February 1900. Slayton—the bad guy—skipped out of the hotel and the city but made the mistake of forgetting his laundry. He telegrammed the hotel requesting that his laundry be forwarded to him in New York. A week later, he was arrested in Buffalo.

There were lawsuits, too, including the one filed on February 9, 1897. Mrs. Laura B. Dowden, Lewis Ginter's housekeeper of three and a half years, sued Ginter and Ginter's niece, Grace Arents, for $25,000 for defamation of character. Various jewelry, silver and money had been missing for some time at Ginter's house, and after an 1896 Christmas Eve ball, more jewelry was discovered missing. Items stolen were primarily from secret drawers in the furniture. The money stolen had been marked but was not recovered. Miss Arents confronted Mrs. Dowden and fired her, saying, according to Dowden, that Ginter thought she was the thief. The theft was reported to the police. Detective Charles Gibson searched the servants' effects while they were sleeping. In Mrs. Dowden's presence, he searched her belongings. Nothing was found. Dowden then hired Mr. Wendenberg to represent her. She offered to drop the charges if Ginter denied making the accusation and Arents apologized. Through their attorney, Charles Stringfellow, Ginter denied having accused Dowden of being dishonest, and Arents claimed Dowden had misunderstood her. But Arents would not apologize. Dowden claimed she had witnesses to prove Arents and Ginter had accused her of stealing.

Originally set for July 1897, the trial got postponed because Ginter's physician ordered him to go to a health resort. Amidst the upcoming trial, Lewis Ginter died on October 2, 1897, a little before the second anniversary of the opening of his hotel. When the trial finally occurred, Grace Arents was the only defendant. There were five witnesses at the trial: Arents, Arents's sister, Mrs. Dowden and two character witnesses for Dowden (Reverend Pike Powers, the rector of St. Andrews Church, and Mary Wilkinson). Arents and her sister testified that Arents did not accuse Dowden of stealing. Dowden stated that Arents had told two others—Powers and Wilkinson—that Dowden had stolen the items. After a two-day, "very stubbornly fought" trial, the jury awarded $1,000 to Mrs. Dowden.

To get an idea what $1,000 was worth at the time, consider that The Jefferson Hotel's net earnings for the entire year of 1900 were $63,921.79, or about $175 per day. Net earnings for the first three months of 1901, before the fire, were $28,019.95.

II

A Day of Sorrow
in Richmond

Then came the big tragedy on Friday, March 29, 1901. The fire
started at about 9:30 p.m. in a fourth-floor blanket room in the
southeast corner of the building. A bellboy noticed that electric lights in
that part of the hotel were out. He notified James Booker, the chief clerk.
Booker put out the fire, or at least thought he had. As Booker went back
downstairs, the fire continued out of view between the ceiling and the
floor above. By 11:00 p.m., it was obvious that a fire was blazing. One
witness later recounted, "All of us stood around silently and watched the
fire. Some had tears in their eyes. The hotel had become the center of
social life in the years before the fire, and no visit to the city was complete
without an inspection of it."

There were about three hundred guests in the hotel at the time,
including R.J. Reynolds of Winston, North Carolina, and Captain
Parker, formerly of the U.S. Navy, who escaped in his evening clothes,
concealed by an overcoat. All that was with him was burned in the fire.
Henry Baskerville, who had recently moved to the hotel, lost everything.
Mr. Sheppard, who ran the cigar stand, barely got out: "I was trying to
save what I could and get my cash when the roof fell in. All around it
rained fire and smoke."

The hotel's insurance of $540,000 consisted of $15,000 for boilers;
$15,000 for dynamos; $13,000 for miscellaneous items, including liquor,
cigars and tobacco; $112,000 for furniture, beds, carpets, linen, plates,
china, silver and paintings; and $385,000 for the hotel building, including

doors, windows, clock towers, electric wiring, Russian baths and elevators. In addition, The Jefferson Statue was insured for $15,000.

Incredibly, guests took their time leaving the hotel during the fire, annoying the firemen. George Wilson didn't leave his room until twenty minutes after first hearing the noise and seeing smoke. He later claimed that a hotel employee told him "there was no occasion for excitement and not until the ceiling was broken and the flames shot through from the floor above...did I think it time for me to get out." A fireman was quoted as saying:

> *The guests of the hotel got in our way. Instead of getting out of the hotel, they stood around and crowded us until the place got so hot they had to get out...We had to pull some of the guests out of their rooms and force them to leave, and it is the greatest wonder in the world that there was not many more casualties...The guests did not seem to think the fire would amount to much. They had the greatest confidence in our ability to stop it, but we realized that a big fight was ahead of us, and we wanted to get those guests out of our way.*

Manager Fry's wife and three children were in the hotel when the fire started. Their belongings were destroyed by the water. The next day, March 30, was "a day of sorrow in Richmond...long will those who saw the hotel go down in destruction recall the harrowing sight and remember their emotions as it crumbled to ruins." Years later, another paper summarized the sorrow: "When the first pearly streaks of dawn lighted the horizon, all that remained of The Jefferson Hotel was its tottering walls, a few blackened chimneys, and the major portion of its Franklin Street front. The rest of the exquisite structure was a chaotic mass of smoking ashes." The intense heat kept firemen there for days. The fire occurred on a Friday night, but firemen were still pouring water on the ruins the following Monday. Richmonders read about one heroic scene:

> *Meanwhile the crowd below held their breath as the two men made their perilous descent. For a moment their comrades below ceased their work of fighting the flames that now had spread over the entire building. It seemed an age from the moment they left the window until they alighted on terra firma, although, as a matter of fact, the descent probably did not consume a minute and a half. When they*

were about 20 feet from the ground, the crowd below broke loose and shouted themselves hoarse in pure excess of joy at the daring escape of Boswell and Frank.

Boswell and Frank were firemen who made a miraculous escape by climbing down a fire hose, witnessed by the thousands who had come out to view the tragedy. One report estimated that nine-tenths of the people of Richmond watched the fire.

John Jaspers, the preacher who often performed his "Sun Do Move" sermon at the hotel, died on March 30, 1901. The *Richmond Dispatch* commented, "It is a sad coincidence that the destruction of The Jefferson Hotel and the death of the Rev. John Jaspers have fallen upon the same day. John Jaspers was a Richmond institution, as surely so as was Major Ginter's fine hotel."

Richmond writer Ellen Glasgow lost her manuscript for a novel she was writing about the Civil War. She had given it for typing to Julia McRae, the hotel's stenographer. McRae went home that day and left the handwritten manuscript in her office. Glasgow ended up publishing the book—*The Battle-Ground*—early in 1904.

A month before the fire, one of the largest carpet contracts ever arranged in Richmond was awarded by The Jefferson Hotel Company to the Cohen Company, to cover the three great dining rooms with the finest Biglow Wilton carpet. Three weeks before the fire, Joseph Willard of Fairfax County joined his family at the hotel for his campaign to become lieutenant governor of Virginia (he won). Two weeks before the fire, it had been reported that The Jefferson was "overrun with wealthy tourists." A week before the fire, forty-five additional bathrooms were completed inside the hotel. Two days before the fire, it was reported that business was so good that The Jefferson Hotel Company declared a 1 percent stock dividend, the first ever: "The hotel seems never to have been so popular, and is doing the largest business in its career."

After the Fire

Construction matters aside, the hotel was left with a host of issues to resolve in the fire's wake. All the hotel's valuable pottery had been stolen after the fire, leading Manager Fry to diplomatically make a public plea:

An 1897 letter. Note the additional charge for a room with a bath. *Courtesy of George Ross.*

used in The Jefferson—so science works inside of beauty and art." Two sculptured large lions guarded the Rotunda at the foot of the staircase. Rates started at $1.50 per day, a dollar more with a private bath.

Another advertisement from this period shows six hand-drawn views of the hotel with a tranquil marketing blurb next to each area of the hotel.

In the reception parlor, "room succeeds room in charming variety." The Rotunda was said to be "like the ante-chamber of a palace." A view from Main Street proclaimed, "A good idea is here afforded of its extent." On the roof garden, "art and nature combine to make time bring sweet content." A meal in the dining room "will always leave a fragrant recollection," and of the Jefferson Statue, the blurb said, "Simplicity pervades the whole scene."

Myers and Hedian Art Company of Baltimore displayed "an extremely choice collection of water colors and artist proof etchings," and Mrs. Preston exhibited and sold miniature paintings, one portraying Governor Andrew Jackson Montague. But the granddaddy of the art sales occurred over five days starting on November 12, 1906, when Miss Fletcher showed her collection, which included Leonardo da Vinci's *L'Annonciation* (for the princely sum of $100); three Rembrandts, priced at $400, $100 and $50; two Titians, one for $200 and the other for $20; and Goya's *Portrait de M. de Castro*, priced at $20.

Horses were a big topic. In those years, Richmond hosted an annual horse show each fall. The society pages regularly reported on out-of-towners making the trip for the show. Mrs. Roger Pryor of New York stayed at The Jefferson during the 1902 show, as did the recently married Mr. and Mrs. Charles H. Consolvo of Norfolk. A few years down the road, Mr. Consolvo would go on to own the hotel. Mrs. G.V. Barnum and Mr. Zenus F. Barnum saw the ponies in Richmond in October 1904 and stayed at The Jefferson Hotel.

Some animals even made an appearance inside the hotel. In April 1903, a chimpanzee named Counsel gave a public reception, smoking cigars and pipes, which he could light himself. This multitalented marvel also performed tricycle tricks (including riding one seven different ways) and could write with pen and paper. Counsel was fond of dogs but "a sworn enemy to cats." He wouldn't associate with monkeys. His antics, the newspaper reported, "would make a dumb man laugh aloud. He can do anything that a man can do except talk." Also performing were acts known as Bonavita and His Lions and Madame Morelli and Her Leopards.

Other interesting specimens at The Jefferson were the college men who played football for the University of Virginia and the Virginia Polytechnic Institute (VPI). These rivals, "the best two teams of the South," played in October 1904 in Richmond, with the players staying at the hotel. The VPI players averaged about 165 pounds each. "They were taken to their training table, where they were given a frugal supper especially adopted to the development of athletes. The boys are a heafy [*sic*] and robust lot."

Another hefty and robust man you might have seen in the fall of 1904 was "Honest John McLean." This 250-pound man, who was born in France, had just opened a free soup kitchen at the Nineteenth Street Mission. He did all the cooking himself. The story stated that he had formerly held a high position at The Jefferson and had also worked at the Alcazar Hotel in St. Augustine, Florida (St. Augustine again).

This wasn't too long after James J. Jeffries, an "undefeated pugilist and base-ball umpire," arrived in Richmond and stayed at The Jefferson. While in town, he umpired a game between the Richmond Jimplecutes [*sic*] and a team from Petersburg. He also gave an exhibition in the "fistic arts" with a sparring partner. Jeffries, the heavyweight champion from 1899 to 1905, was considered a giant in his day. He stood six feet, one inch tall and weighed 225 pounds.

One especially interesting wedding at the hotel was between two New Yorkers, Dr. Harry Rodman (sometimes referred to as Dr. Henry Heth Rodman) and Miss Edith Wyman, a nurse. The *New York Evening World* reported that Rodman was from a distinguished Virginia family. They were childhood friends. He had served on the hospital ship *Maine* during the Boer War. Many newspapers around the country picked up this love story. The *Atlanta Constitution* called the July 1902 wedding "the most romantic and unusual as ever accompanied a union." Suffering at the time from scarlet fever, he had come to Virginia for his health. When he got extremely ill, he sent for her. He was so ill during the wedding ceremony, the newspapers reported, that while he was lying in bed, the ceremony had to be temporarily halted several times so oxygen (often referred to in the stories as restoratives) could be applied to him. "Only the immediate relatives of the groom attended the pathetic bridal scene in what threatened to become at any moment a death chamber." The *New York Tribune* stated that the couple left for New York the next day "with the prospect that the bridegroom might be dead before he reached Washington." "Wedded in His Bed at The Jefferson," announced the headline of the *Richmond Times*. "The story leading up to this culmination reads more like the creation of some fertile brain rather than a plain recital of facts."

But confirming once again that you really never know, it turns out that one of them did die shortly afterward, but it wasn't the groom. The bride died of cancer six months later, and the doctor was reported to be in good health since the wedding.

Another fascinating wedding at The Jefferson involved the 1899 Valentine's Day nuptials between a twenty-five-year-old actor named Willard Hutchinson and Mrs. W.H. Marco, whose age, depending on various press accounts, was somewhere between seventy and seventy-eight. As a wedding gift, she gave him—with no adjustment for inflation—$3 million. They both lived in New York. Prior to marrying the much younger Hutchinson, she had just divorced her third husband, a man forty-five years her junior.

After the wedding, the young, raffish actor started drinking and "absented himself," causing her to sue for a separation. That led to a flurry of national stories in 1902. He then threatened to put his new old wife in an asylum, claiming she was insane and suggesting she transfer all her assets to him. He got members of her family to agree to the idea, and before long, the wise woman realized that if she wanted to stay out of an institution, she'd better cut a deal. They brought in lawyers, and everything was settled, including a clause stating that whoever lived longer would end up with all the assets—a pretty good deal for him. But it soon didn't seem so certain after all. The *New York Evening World* carried a story in November 1902 that Hutchinson was near death from an accidental overdose of morphine. He survived and ended up performing in many plays, including *Lottery of Love, When We Were Twenty-One* and a "lively farce" called *The Man from the Hat Shop*. He later married a woman in Washington State in March 1912. The story didn't give her age.

The biggest con against the hotel came by way of a well-connected Washington, D.C. lawyer named Arthur Sinclair Colyar. Colyar (also spelled Colyer or Collyar) stiffed the hotel during horse-show week in October 1902. It was reported that he spent lavishly and gave The Jefferson two checks totaling $219 drawn on the Lincoln National Bank of Washington. He received $146 cash in change. Both checks were worthless. When the law and the hotel caught up with him a year later, he was in a Washington, D.C. prison for an unrelated charge. Just as Colyar was leaving jail after serving five months for that conviction, he was arrested for defrauding The Jefferson a year earlier. In "Arthur Colyer's Escapades" on December 22, 1903, the *New York Sun* reported that Colyer was turned over to Virginia authorities pursuant to Governor Montague's request. In March 1904, Colyar got one year in jail for passing a spurious draft, a grand larceny charge.

REBUILDING THE HOTEL

Even at half a hotel, business was humming along pretty well in early 1903. Indeed, the half hotel was doing so well that it was turning away many people because of lack of space. Some of the guests who did get rooms included "the distinguished New York journalist, Murat Halstead," whose name, according to one obsequious piece, "is known from one end of the land to the other...his years sit lightly upon his shoulders...his clever and entertaining address won him a host of new admirers." Mr. and Mrs. Schuyler Hamilton of New York stayed for several weeks. It was reported in July 1903 that they had moved out of the hotel and bought a house at 815 West Franklin Street. A few months later, on March 29, 1904, Mr. W.P. Tams, a well-known Staunton banker, stayed at the hotel on the third anniversary of the fire. He had been a guest the night of the fire.

Rebuilding the hotel was not an easy or sure thing. Manager Fry was asked in September 1903 if the hotel would be rebuilt, and all he could say was that he hadn't heard anything at all on the subject. One of the Richmond papers reported, "Jefferson Will Not Be Rebuilt." The decision was up to George Arents, the principal owner, who was traveling in Europe. Arents, Ginter's nephew, had taken over ownership of the hotel after Lewis Ginter died. Someone asked George Arents (when he returned to his Manhattan residence from travel abroad) about rebuilding the burned part of the hotel, and Arents claimed total indifference, saying he hadn't talked to anyone about it and hadn't given it any thought. In the fall of 1903, George Mayo auctioned 350,000 to 400,000 high-grade bricks from The Jefferson, not something you'd do if planning a renovation. Arents didn't appear to have any inclination to rebuild.

This uncertainty was pushing Manager Fry to look elsewhere for employment. What respectable hotel man would want to run half a hotel with the uncertainty of not knowing when things would improve? He might have been sending a message to Arents that he would seek other employment if The Jefferson didn't get rebuilt. A story in August 1904 reported that Fry had just returned from "the famous Toxaway County of Western North Carolina—where he visited five magnificent hotels." Fires are always a bad thing, especially if they occur when deciding whether to rebuild from an earlier fire. While Arents was debating, a small fire burned on May 14, 1903, in the hotel's airshaft.

A Day of Sorrow in Richmond

The fire department quickly extinguished the blaze, which was believed to have been caused by "spontaneous combustion, the heat from the furnaces of the hotel and the sun igniting a lot of accumulated grease."

Rather than rebuild the hotel, Arents sold it. The Jefferson Realty Corporation purchased The Jefferson Hotel and associated property for $307,000 ($300,000 for the building and $7,000 for the adjoining lot) in April 1905. George Arents and Thomas Jeffress, trustees of Ginter's estate, also transferred the additional 82 feet adjacent to the hotel fronting Main Street for another $17,300. The building that had been on this lot was crushed during the fire by falling walls. The prospectus reported the hotel fronted 144 feet, 2 inches of Main Street; 309 feet, 8 inches on Jefferson Street; and 145 feet on Franklin. A company in Milwaukee, Wisconsin, had valued the building and its equipment in 1904 at $692,721.54, with an additional $75,000 for the land.

Hotel business had been steadily improving. Net profits were $15,747.56 for 1903 and $12,683.00 for 1904. For just the first four months of 1905, profits stood at $10,444.67. The *Times Dispatch* predicted in March 1905 that the hotel would be rebuilt "more grandly" than before. It heavily credited David Lowenberg of Norfolk as being the driving force among the new owners. For the purchase and reconstruction, the State Corporation Commission granted a charter to The Jefferson Realty Corporation for $1.4 million of preferred and common stock. Newspaper notices appeared in July 1905 offering shares in the new corporation. The Virginia Trust Company handled the sale of a sizable portion, including 250 shares to Captain P.H. Mayo; 100 to Lancaster & Lucke; 50 each to the Virginia Fire & Marine Insurance Company and to Davenport & Company; 30 to Caroline Colten; 10 to Mrs. S.V. Graves; and 6 to John Hunter Jr. Within five months, The Jefferson's own Joseph Willard, who was also Virginia's lieutenant governor, became a member of the State Corporation Commission, replacing a resigning member. "It is understood," the story reported, "that Captain Willard disposed of all his railroad stocks and will resign as lieutenant governor tomorrow.

The principal members of The Jefferson Realty Corporation were Joseph Bryan, president; Joseph Willard, first vice-president; David Lowenberg, second vice-president; and James Dooley. The first meeting of the new corporation began at 5:15 p.m. on April 20, 1905, in Bryan's office.

Joseph Bryan was born in Gloucester County, Virginia, on April 13, 1845. He served briefly in the Civil War with the Richmond Howitzers and later Mosby's Rangers. In October 1864, the month he joined Mosby's Rangers, he was wounded twice near Upperville, Virginia. He owned the Richmond Locomotive and Machine Works, which at its peak employed three thousand workers. In 1887, he purchased the *Richmond Times* and later the *Richmond Dispatch*. He merged both papers in 1903. In 1908, he acquired the *Richmond News Leader*, which gave him control of both of Richmond's major daily papers. He died in November 1908 and is buried at Emmanuel Episcopal Church.

Joseph Edward Willard was born on May 1, 1865, in Washington, D.C. He was elected lieutenant governor of Virginia in 1901, a position he held until September 30, 1905, when appointed to the State Corporation Commission. When the Spanish-American War broke out, he organized and equipped at his own expense an infantry company. The unit was mustered into the army. He had varied leadership interests, including ownership of the Richmond and Rappahannock Railroad and acting as president of the Bank of Commerce and Trusts, ambassador to Spain and principal stockholder of the Willard Hotel in Washington, D.C. He died in 1924.

David Lowenberg was born in Germany on October 25, 1839. He came to America in 1855, arriving at New York, before eventually migrating to South Carolina. He served in the Sixteenth South Carolina Infantry Regiment during the Civil War. After the war, he moved to Norfolk and went into business and eventually owned the Lowenberg Boot & Shoe Company, which at one time was the largest shoe store in the Norfolk area. He eventually got involved in many businesses—banks, cotton manufacturing, minerals, real estate and railroads—before becoming the principal owner of the Monticello Hotel in Norfolk. He was director of the 1907 Jamestown Exposition, an event that directly led to The Jefferson reopening when it did in 1907.

James H. Dooley was born in Richmond on January 17, 1841. He served under his father during the Civil War in the First Virginia Regiment. A serious wound of his right wrist at the Battle of Williamsburg resulted in a major lifelong deformity. He was captured and released and later served as a lieutenant in the reserve corps. He was called major but never achieved that rank. It's likely the title was informally given to him because his father had been a major. After the war, he practiced law. He retired from law in 1899 to run various business ventures, including the

Seaboard Air Line Railway System. As of 1890, he was reported to be one of four thousand millionaires in the United States. Dooley died in November 1922 and was originally buried at Hollywood Cemetery. His body was later moved to a mausoleum at Maymont, his Richmond home.

PUTTING THE TEAM TOGETHER[2]

Joseph Bryan wrote to a man named W.C. Bentley of Richmond, denying his request to become an officer in the business: "My Dear Willie: It would give me the greatest pleasure to have you associated with me in any way…but there will be no paid secretary and treasurer of The Jefferson Hotel for a long time. The present officers are acting without any salary."

David Lowenberg seemed to be waffling on his commitment to invest heavily. Bryan had to make this pitch to keep him aboard:

> *I cannot help feeling some little anxiety about the matter as it is plain to me that the question of the continuance of The Jefferson Realty Corporation is involved…You well understand that none of the Richmond gentlemen went into this business as a mere matter of making money. It was to build The Jefferson Hotel that they were induced to make the subscription.*

The new owners retained Keevan Peebles of Norfolk as the principal architect. For $4,000, they also locked in New York architects Clinton & Russell for consulting and design services. For a superintendent, debate ensued about hiring a man named Baskerville for an amount that seemed too low to believe for Joseph Bryan: "As to the employment of Mr. Baskerville, I question if he would be gotten for $100 or $125 per month, and a man at that price would not be the man to give confidence to our people that should be required…In addition to the superintendent there is usually a clerk of the work who gets $100 or $125 a month." One critical decision was whether to stay with five-bedroom floors or add a sixth. Bryan favored six.

Architect Peebles went to New York to inspect hotels in the summer of 1905 and get some ideas. Lowenberg and Manager Fry followed

---

2. Most of Joseph Bryan's correspondence comes from his letterbook at the Virginia Historical Society.

a couple months later. Bryan also eventually went north to check out the Astor Hotel, built by Clinton & Russell. He spent about two hours investigating it from roof garden to the boiler floor and opined that its layout was splendid. "The machinery part is superbly done, and they have an arrangement there where the visitors can walk back and look through large panes of glass upon a brilliant electrical apparatus room." Bryan preferred that The Jefferson's walls be papered rather than painted. He remarked that painted walls were desirable in cases of contagious epidemic, but "we are not building a hospital." He added five other suggestions: 1) The Jefferson should have a roof garden like the Astor; 2) the ladies' café should be kept where it was, opening on the palm garden, and the children and nurses located somewhere else; 3) the hotel should install an observation place for the machinery; 4) the rooms should be arranged to easily accommodate guests' personal servants so that long-term guests could have their servants stay with them at reasonable rates; and 5) the bedroom windows should have inside blinds to turn back in what are known as box frames, so as not to interfere with the curtains ("this is an exceedingly important feature in our climate, where you have to get the air and at the same time keep out the sun").

The hotel would get a newly designed auditorium to hold eight hundred people. The Jefferson Street façade was to be removed, and a handsome entrance with a massive façade would grace the Main Street entrance. The entrance to the foyer would be from the center of Main Street. In September 1905, it was reported that renovations had started and were expected to cost nearly $1,000,000. The contactor promised the work would be completed within a year.

They had to make all kinds of decisions. Lowenberg sent Bryan two contracts between the hotel and the barbers who leased the shop. The P.F. Corbin Company of New Britain, Connecticut (local Richmond agent: Watkins-Cotrell Company), got the contract to provide finishing hardware. Bryan advised a man named William M. Jenkins that the board would consider installing an Estey organ.

The contract for lobby fixtures, dining room chairs and rathskeller fixtures came down to either E.B. Shaw & Company of Boston or the Sloan Company of New York. Shaw eventually got selected. Bryan let Lowenberg know that he wasn't "much concerned about the balance," as he felt "no anxiety about our not getting satisfactory furniture for a fair price." It appears Sloan furnished the carpets and mattresses.

Deciding on the marble led to correspondence on whether to get it from Tennessee or Georgia. Bryan pushed for Tennessee marble, which cost $868 more. Lowenberg spelled out the factors to consider: "The preference of Georgia marble over Tennessee is a mere matter of taste and if the Georgia harmonizes with our scagliola better than the Tennessee, we should have Georgia." They had to select the contractor to supply and install the systems handling steam, heating, ventilation and the power plant. The proposals came down to five contractors with prices ranging from $19,314 to $27,400. Three of the bidders were from New York. The winning bidder was the low one: the Morrison Machinery & Supply Company.

Like in any big construction project, there were a lot of problems. The 300th Anniversary Jamestown Exposition was coming up, something the hotel hoped to cash in on by attracting guests passing near Richmond. Unfortunately, the exposition pulled workers, creating a labor shortage at The Jefferson, a problem frequently remarked upon in news accounts, including the following blurb in the *Hotel Monthly* in 1907: "The completion of the new Jefferson Hotel is delayed on account of the scarcity of mechanics, the Jamestown Exposition having practically drained Richmond of its skilled labor."

Once The Jefferson got enough workers, there were problems with pay. Bricklayers went on strike to demand a raise, from twenty and a half cents to twenty-five cents an hour. It appears there was no agreement because Bryan ended up threatening the painting contractor, William Baumgartner & Company of New York: "I regret to learn…that your painters have been called out by their union…and that he is now without men to carry out the contract, and is unable to continue his work. As this hotel is to be opened positively on the fifth of May, I have no alternative but to adopt such means…to have the work completed." Bryan was justifiably worried. The renovation project was looking less than propitious. "We will not have The Jefferson Hotel done on time by a long shot," Bryan sternly warned, "if we don't take hold of it actively and vigorously." He notified John T. Wilson, a Richmond general contractor, to start paint and decorative work if Baumgartner did not resume work by the morning of April 22. Baumgartner did not get started on time, and Wilson ended up doing the work. Lawsuits followed, but we'll get to that later.

In the midst of all the difficulties in rebuilding, the owners had a few personal issues too. In January 1906, Bryan's house burned down, leaving us to reflect on the cruel irony: while investing his fortune and time to rebuild a hotel that had burned, his house suffered the same fiery fate. The rules of etiquette demanded that friends express their sympathy, and the Bryans were to respond with appropriate acknowledgment. Hotel Manager Fry offered his thoughts, and the Bryans responded in a preprinted card: "Mr. and Mrs. Joseph Bryan desire to return their thanks to <u>Mr. Fry</u> for <u>his</u> gratifying expression of sympathy upon the burning of Laburnum. Brook Hill, Va." Bryan ended up rebuilding Laburnum.

Lowenberg was not involved in a fire but may have just missed the Great San Francisco Earthquake of 1906. He had found the time to make a trip out west, but it's not known whether it was to scout out ideas for the hotel or for pleasure; either way, he was out there about the time of the disaster, prompting Bryan to write, "I rejoice to believe that you and Mrs. Lowenberg escaped from San Francisco before the great calamity which has befallen it."

There were two known casualties at The Jefferson during the renovation. On March 20, 1906, a twenty-seven-year-old riveter named E.J. Martin fell sixty-five feet from the fourth floor. The other casualty during the rebuilding was thirty-two-year-old Samuel Clinton Hulce, who died on November 1, 1905, in a freak elevator accident. He had gone to the hotel to get an account straightened out for his father, Captain E.P. Hulce, of the Second Station Police Department. Before the accident, the partially deaf Hulce had stopped to say hello to W.H. Lee, the hotel steward. It was believed he hit his head in a six-foot fall in the elevator. The elevator boy heard a strange sound, like a body falling. He reported it to Mr. C.D. Proffit, the hotel carpenter, who reported it to Clerk Oscar Weisiger. The *Times Dispatch* carried a picture of Hulce. Coincidentally, The Jefferson took out an advertisement ten months later to sell two fully equipped elevators. It had planned all along to replace the elevators as part of the renovation.

The board of directors reported that there had been setbacks during the renovation, but things were looking good. "It is the purpose of your directors," the report proclaimed,

> *that this hotel shall in every respect maintain the reputation of The Jefferson Hotel for elegance and every convenience...The processes of construction have interrupted materially the ordinary operations of the hotel and yet, despite inconvenience and noise, the hotel has been*

A Day of Sorrow in Richmond

well patronized, and for a part of the time has been overcrowded…the demand for such a hotel as this seems to be increasing every day.

The new Jefferson would have about four hundred bedrooms, nearly all of which, the board proudly added "will be directly accessible to bathrooms."

In the end, the box scores read like this, from information obtained from board of director reports: Corporation treasurer Oliver J. Sands reported that $1,008,165.76 had been paid for the hotel and for rebuilding it, boasting that the hotel was appraised at $692,000, but they got it for $300,000. In addition, the new owners "obtained the goodwill of a hotel whose reputation for elegance and excellence was spread abroad throughout the country." The priceless and hard-to-quantify asset called goodwill was put at "the very moderate valuation of $58,000, less than half the cost of the advertising." As for some other assets, cash on hand stood at $26,590.07. The owners valued the movable furniture at $79,929.95 and determined the carpets and hangings were worth $33,075.48.

Payments to John T. Wilson were expected to total $451,844. But that did not include the mechanical plant or the ornamental plastering work, which would be an additional $10,000. Wilson's daughter would live at the hotel and end up getting involved with a cult leader in Missouri. But that's decades later and several chapters away.

Peebles was paid $17,500.00, less a $500.00 rebate for the mechanical engineer and less another $1,500.00 for the building superintendent, who was physically on hotel grounds at all times. Clinton & Russell got the agreed-upon $4,000.00; Morrison Machinery received $19,314.36 for steam heating and the piping plant and $6,950.00 for engine and repairing the ice machine. Dwyer Heating & Plumbing received $6,000.00; Sanitary Device Manufacturing Company, $3,840.00, for vacuum cleaning plant; P.F. Corbin Hardware, $1,080.00; Electric Construction Company, $19,071.00; Otis Elevator, $13,500.00, for three elevators (two passenger and one freight); and Wrought Iron Range Company of St. Louis, $3,000.00. Wilhelm & Company received $21,359.00 for ornamental plastering work, as well as three additional payments of $650.00 each for work that was not identified.

The hotel got hit with wave after wave of lawsuits. A plethora of stories mentioned the various lawsuits involving The Jefferson Hotel Company (JHC). One reported that the courts were going to merge eighteen different cases into one titled *Frank Brumbaugh and Others v.*

The Jefferson Hotel Company. Frank Brumbaugh sued, claiming that JHC was responsible for the delay in his not completing work on time. In his suit, Brumbaugh claimed that the total amount owed to him and his subcontractors was $67,767.30. About $30,000.00 had been paid, leaving an outstanding balance of $37,518.36. The JHC countersued Brumbaugh for $12,000.00, claiming that the delay was his fault. After the deadline, Brumbaugh was supposed to pay a $150.00 daily penalty. A mechanic named W.F. Eberman filed suit for $42.25 for work, which was to be paid at thirty and a half cents an hour. Lemuel Cole claimed he was owed $56.75, representing 227 hours worked at twenty-five cents an hour. Joseph and Charles Shur combined their court filings into a total claim of $469.50, calculated from Joseph's daily pay of $21.00 and the $13.50 that Charles was owed. Messrs. C.H. Maloney and Edward Collins of Elkhart, Indiana, filed suit against the JHC for $15,444.04 in plumbing and electrical work, and the Dietrick Brothers of Baltimore claimed $2,136.60 for ironwork. The National Mantel and Tile Company of Baltimore filed suit against both the JHC and Brumbaugh for $2,875.00 for fireproofing, which was completed in December 1901. The Southern Asbestos Manufacturing Company sued Maloney and Collins for $91.67. Mr. H.C. Lynn sued Maloney/Collins, as well as the JHC, and a Mr. W.S. Gunn hit the legal trifecta, suing three entities: JHC, Brumbaugh and George Arents. Morrison Machinery & Supply Company also sued the hotel. To Mr. Hackley Morrison, Bryan wrote, "I regret to learn that you have undertaken legal proceedings to avert the company's doing that which in my opinion, you ought to have done yourself as soon as the judgment of the architect was given."

The decision came out in May 1908. After reviewing and considering 1,200 pages of evidence, the court ordered the JHC to pay $37,000 to Brumbaugh and the others. The JHC appealed and learned in June 1909 that it had lost the appeal. The U.S. Court of Appeals denied rehearing the Brumbaugh case.

The Maloney/Collins case against The Jefferson, which had not been combined with Brumbaugh, was settled out of court.

III

The Jefferson Reopens

The new design left the Grand Staircase uncovered by an arch. The Jefferson Realty Corporation leased out the Cigar & News stand for $100 a month during hotel construction and $250 per month after construction was completed. The business had turned a $62 average monthly profit by the previous owners. Nothing had been done by 1905 about leasing the drugstore, florist shop, ladies' hair dressing establishment, haberdashery or barbershop.

Mr. A.J. Wolverton leased the Turkish baths for $200 a month. The baths had averaged $242 monthly in profits over the prior nine months. Professor Wolverton bought a notice touting his extensive experience and advertising that he had just arrived from New York. The baths having been thoroughly renovated, anyone could get a massage, swimming lessons or electric and sulphur treatments. Physical culture and chiropody were available, but the ad didn't explain what that meant. And if you had a problem with ingrown toenails, they'd take care of that, too.

The country was going through a severe economic depression, something that would hurt hotel business. The board of directors' report ended on a somber note: "It must be said, however, that the opening of the year, as indicated by the month of January just closed, has shown in our business the effect of the depression which prevails throughout our country. Travel has not been as great as we expected, and the money is not spent as freely."

On May 6, 1907, the hotel reopened after the fire. Yes, it had been running pretty much continuously (with the exception of one year), but in 1907, the entire hotel opened. The new owners had spent considerable money to bring it to the high standards set by Lewis Ginter.

The hotel reopened in time for the Jamestown Exposition and the Episcopalians. Joseph Bryan had personally guaranteed that Richmond would be ready to host the annual convention of the Episcopal Church, which started on October 1, 1907.

The hotel wasn't reopened at the time of the funeral of Varina Davis, Jefferson Davis's widow. History records the funeral procession to Hollywood Cemetery on October 20, 1906, as an epic day in Richmond. By the way, a few papers, like the *Carbondale* [Illinois] *Free Press*, had incorrectly reported that The Jefferson Hotel was named for Jefferson Davis.

Things picked up quickly. The biggest change might have been that the hotel was now often referred to as the *New* Jefferson Hotel, the word "new" a welcome descriptor to help potential guests determine which of the country's Jefferson Hotels was the one in Richmond. In the first few decades of the twentieth century, there were no fewer than thirty-eight hotels named for Thomas Jefferson, including three each in New York, Texas and Florida and two each in New Jersey, California, Illinois, Iowa, Indiana, Ohio, Georgia and Alabama. As you would expect, Virginia, with five, had the most hotels named for the author of the Declaration of Independence. As a play on that historical significance, The Jefferson—the one in Richmond—put out a pamphlet entitled *The Declaration of Independence to the Tourist and Traveler*, which began:

> *When in the course of human events it becomes necessary for the people who travel in search of health or pleasure, or on business, to dissolve the bands that have held them to wretched hotels, and caused them on their journeys South to avoid the beautiful historic City of Richmond, though directly on the route, a decent respect for the opinion of the public requires that they should have good reasons to impel them to a separation. We hold these truths to be self-evident; that the traveling public are endowed with certain inalienable rights, that among these are life, so surrounded with comfort and luxury as to be a pleasure rather than a burden, liberty to feel they can visit any locality and find modern hotel accommodations, and the pursuit of happiness so provided for as to be more than a bit of rhetoric.*

Historical and marketing documents aside, we're back to the operation of the hotel where, as usual, performers entertained. Harold Bauer gave a piano recital in February 1908. "He has given concerts during the past few years in so many continental cities," one newspaper reported, "that an admirer has laughingly suggested that Bauer's fame rests quite as much upon his record as a traveler, as upon his skill as a musician."

Also putting on piano demonstrations were E. Leslie Loth, a nineteen-year-old Richmond man, and Miss Minnie Derby, "Richmond's brilliant young pianist." Those who enjoyed listening to fine musicians might also have heard the Italian Boys, whose group included a violin, flute, clarinet and harp. For fifty cents, you could see the Whitney Brothers, "America's Greatest Male Quartette."

The Virginia Polytechnic Institute (VPI) alumni held a "smoker" in February 1908. Governor Swanson was supposed to give the address, but it was later reported that he did not attend. At The Jefferson on the same day as the VPI smoker, Richmond's own May Handy—then known as Mrs. James Brown Potter—was posing as Sleeping Beauty in a charity event called "The Indoor Garden Party." For three days in March 1908, The Jefferson Orchestra played two concerts a day at Miller & Rhoads.

The Rotunda after the 1907 rebuilding. *Courtesy of The Jefferson Hotel.*

Just about every group you can imagine convened. Descendants of Thomas Jefferson met in 1908, as did more than one thousand former Confederate soldiers. Paul Revere's grandson attended a convention with his group, the Old Dominion Pilgrims. In combination with the American Political Science Association, the American Historical Association held its twenty-fourth annual conference in 1908. Six hundred farmers cultivated personal and business relations at the fifth annual convention of the State Farmers' Institute in August 1908, and the Tobacco Dealers & Manufacturers had a smoker, with entertainment by Polk Miller and His Famous Negro Quartet. Folks who dealt in fabric wouldn't cotton being left out, so four hundred members of the American Cotton Manufacturers' Association met in May 1909 at their thirteenth annual convention. Other business-directed organizations included the Virginia Hotel Men's Association, which voted for Charles Consolvo to replace Peter Fry as its president. The group reported that one of its most important goals included getting new laws to protect it from deadbeats and unscrupulous and incompetent employees.

Representatives at the January 1909 conference of the Hotel Men's Association of Virginia and North Carolina got a firsthand demonstration of something called the "slot machine typewriter." The Jefferson was one of the first hotels in America to have this new invention, but since they were in scarce supply, the hotel initially got only two. By simply dropping a dime into the machine, guests could type for twenty minutes. "Everyday guests," the press release noted, "are in need of machines on which to write confidential letters which they do not care to dictate to a steno." A hotel guest could request to have one of the machines sent to his room. A topic of discussion at the meeting concerned better cooperation between Virginia and North Carolina in dealing with "flashers," the con men who passed bogus checks and eluded authorities by going back and forth between the two states.

For financial matters, the Richmond branch of the Virginia Banker's Association hosted a smoker, with subsequent reports claiming, "The jollification lasted well into the night." Perhaps the jolliest get-together of all occurred on Christmas Eve 1909 with a fun-loving bunch who didn't take themselves too seriously. They called their activity "The Fifth Annual Tour" and dedicated it to the "jolliest bunch of flint-hearted monologists whose tongues ever prattled idle gossip." The song sheet included "Hail, Hail, the Gang's All Here" and "There'll Be a

Hot Time in the Old Town To-night." The dinner menu was listed like acts in a play, and the setting—"Sanctum Sanctorum"—was The Jefferson. The group included a humorous section in the program, called "Candidates for Departure with Dates," which jokingly predicted when and how they might eventually die. Miss Mary Bright, "inclined to pudginess," was to make it only to the next year, 1910. Miss Mary Gold, "lovely Mary—extremely thin," to 1911; Miss Bruce Ferneyhough, "of uncertain age," to 1912; and Miss Hazel Bright, with the biographical remark of "whew, what a temper!" to 1913. Also included in the group were Miss Anne Lecky, Miss Mary Wooldridge and Dr. Fulmer Bright.

It's likely these partiers were able to take swigs of alcohol. Prohibition may have been years away, but anti-drinking ordinances were front and center at the time. In February 1907, The Jefferson was fined $100 for violating the Umlauf Law, named for a hard-charging temperance politician. By January 1908, the hotel had received an exemption from the Dabney Ordinance, which declared that no license would be granted to any establishment with which shows or concerts were connected. The hotel successfully argued that its hall was used for lectures and recitals, as well as concerts. The ordinance was eventually amended "so the leading hotels would not be deprived of the right of supplying [their] guests with liquid refreshments." The Jefferson was one of only five "social clubs" to obtain liquor licenses, but only five applied. The other potential applicants, the newspaper pointed out, understood their applications would be promptly rejected. It appears the hotel was bottling its own liquor. The hotel's museum today has a bottle of Jefferson Whiskey, and a newspaper advertisement from October 1908 touted something called Jefferson Club Whiskey.

The National Wholesale Druggists' Association had its thirty-fifth annual convention in October 1909. The schedule included an automobile ride for the ladies. A month after the druggists left the hotel, a man named Harry Huckins was wishing they were still around to give him some pain medicine. Incredibly, in November 1909, this representative of the Boston Shoe Company broke his ankle while sitting in a chair in his room (686). As he reached back to get a cigarette, he heard something crack. Sure enough, his friend heard it, too. Huckins then realized it was his ankle. Hotel employee Billy Quale, who stayed up for late arrivals, said it was the strangest accident he ever heard of.

A few months earlier, the Medical Society of Virginia conferred, with five hundred members present. At this meeting, forty-five papers were read, including one discussing whether cancer was contagious. The gathering included a luncheon at the Women's Club to honor the society's two female doctors. The society's constitution excluded "quacks, charlatans and those who will not subscribe to a recognized code of professional ethics." Before the luncheon, the women were treated to "a tallyho drive around the city." Driving, at the time, was a highly entertaining novelty.

AUTOMOBILING

The notion that someone would drive one of these new machines to The Jefferson Hotel, or anywhere else for that matter, struck just about everybody as eccentric enough to talk and read about. But the novelty should be no wonder when you consider George Selden received the first patent for a gasoline motor engine (a "road engine") on November 5, 1895, less than a week after The Jefferson opened. In a sense, The Jefferson and the automobile grew up together.

In *The History of Virginia*, published in 1924, the author recalled the first automobiles in his community. "They inspired the citizens with wonder," Richard Morton wrote, "and their horses with terror." In 1906, when automobiles were first licensed in Virginia, there were only 626 of them in the entire state. That number increased to 3,680 in 1909 and to 94,000 by 1919.

Newspapers smitten with this newsworthy topic devoted significant space to these new machines. Stories about conventions regularly mentioned the seemingly obligatory drive around the city. Society notices of who was visiting whom frequently carried the news that they were getting to their location by automobile.

The *Richmond Times Dispatch*, for example, wrote in May 1903 that The Jefferson was quickly regaining its old-time popularity with the traveling public, enough so that many northern tourists stopped at the hotel on their journies back in the spring after wintering in Florida. One story mentioned the amazing exploits of a guy named Hugh Willoughby of Newport, Rhode Island, a daring soul who "had begun automobiling about five years ago." This intrepid sojourner—hold your hats here— drove from Rhode Island to Florida each winter, stopping at The Jefferson on each trip. The story came out in November, a little late in the season to be chasing the sunshine in "such a venturesome journey." During the trip, the story recounted, "The wind whistles shrilly by the ears of the solitary automobilier [*sic*] as he bowls along deserted country roads...The atmosphere in the little tent pitched by the roadside for the night is now and then stiff enough to freeze a thermometer."

In March 1908, two cars left Philadelphia for Savannah, Georgia, a veritable round-the-world venture when you think of the distance and the fact that they were competing on roads that were awful and in cars that were no better. A thirty-horsepower Studebaker Touring car and a forty-horsepower Pullman Roadster completed the first leg—203 miles from Philadelphia to Washington—in the "remarkable time" of sixteen hours. In some places, the bad roads won and temporarily halted the event. Both cars got stuck in the mud in Centerville, Virginia, and needed horses to pull them out. The next planned stop for the drivers and "the two machines" was The Jefferson Hotel.

JOHN D. ROCKEFELLER

In late March 1909, John D. Rockefeller and his entourage, a "retinue consist[ing] of valets, nurses, maids and the like," took a ride through the city. The paper reported, "The machines were out about two hours." Traveling to the Virginia Hot Springs in private cars on the Chesapeake and Ohio (C&O) Railroad, the chilled sojourners stopped in Richmond and rented ten private rooms and a parlor at The Jefferson for several hours to warm up. The *Times Dispatch* reported that Rockefeller liked to visit the city because he knew "Richmond was not a brain-storm town." One of the few people allowed to go up to Rockefeller's room at The Jefferson was Carl Ruehrmund, a local architect who at the time was building a skyscraper in New York for the oil king.

As a matter of Virginia trivia and a fact to help you win a bet someday, John D. Rockefeller Jr.—for his work in restoring Colonial Williamsburg—is one of only four people to be named honorary Virginians. Two of the others are Lafayette, the Revolutionary War hero, and Margaret Thatcher, the former prime minister of England. The fourth will be identified in the upcoming pages.

Rockefeller also said he liked Richmond because "big men could come here for a quiet rest without being disturbed by the morbidly curious."

He had heard that J. Pierpoint Morgan stayed in Richmond for several weeks "without being pestered." Morgan, who traveled to Richmond in 1907 for the Episcopal Convention, had leased for $5,000 a month a fashionable home at 112 East Grace Street.

Many knew, or were getting to know, about the legendary Jefferson, which the *Syracuse Herald* called "probably the most sumptuous of the South." The *Herald* reporter got a tour of The Jefferson by the manager, who made a special point to show off the hotel's ice plant, the electrical equipment and the best smoke-consuming device he had ever seen. "Though the hotel burns the softest coal procurable," the story noted, "the underfed automatic stoker that constitutes the device works so well that the manager defies an observer to watch the top of the chimney and tell whether a fire is burning in the furnaces or not." Little did they or their readers know that a few decades later the hotel would be fined for polluting the Richmond skies.

But rich businessmen weren't by any means the only famous guests. Richmond's own Irene Langhorne—the famous Gibson Girl—traveled to the city, where she was the guest of honor at a Jefferson dinner party in October 1907. Another Langhorne sister—Nancy, married to Waldorf Astor of New York—was mentioned in the papers in May 1910, when she made the trip south to Richmond and stayed at The Jefferson. The Langhorne sisters were notorious for their clever quips and retorts. On the subject of marrying Waldorf Astor, one of the richest men on the planet, Nancy said, "I married beneath me. All women do."

President Teddy Roosevelt visited the city and the hotel in October 1905. The mayor and governor greeted Roosevelt and joined him in a parade ending at The Jefferson. One story reported that he was cheered by one of the largest crowds ever witnessed in Richmond. Kids were let out of school, and fifteen thousand of them lined the parade route. Years later, a writer for the *Richmond Quarterly* provided this firsthand recollection:

> *Teddy Roosevelt came to Richmond in 1905 when I was very small. And of course he was drawn up Monument Avenue. Chief Werner was one of the dignitaries who escorted the President. Doris Werner, the chief's youngest child and my playmate, and I went over to see. We marched with them until they stopped at the old Civil War breastworks; they all got out of their carriages and Doris and I ran*

to her father! He introduced us to Teddy and the President picked both of us up in his arms and gave us a kiss! Boy, were we excited! When I came home some hours later and told my parents, Mama was mortified. I was so dirty—and going up to the President! Papa laughed and said, "Lilly, Teddy Roosevelt would never have picked them up if they'd been clean and polished." But I'm not sure it appeased Mama.

President Taft visited Richmond in November 1909. The breakfast, lunch, hotel rooms and invitations for the party of 250 at The Jefferson cost $3,381.25. President Roosevelt's 1905 visit to Richmond, the story claimed, cost $8,501.10.

A January 1909 advertisement in *Collier's Weekly* touted The Jefferson's "strictly high class restaurant," which served meals on the European plan, not the American plan. Rooms at the "Most Magnificent Hotel in the South" cost "$2.00 and up," an increase of $0.50 over a year earlier. Rates had held steady at "$1.50 and up" since about 1897.

At the end of 1907, the hotel had $9,121.82 in cash on hand. Glass, crockery and cooking utensils were valued at $10,513.63; silverware, at $7,978.67; and bed and table linen, at $19,185.16. The hotel had a net profit that year of $90,901.02. Management also kept track of the number of visitors who stayed one night. The hotel had precisely 56,342 guests who stayed for one night in 1907.

JEFFERSON HOTEL EMPLOYEES IN THE NEWS

Jefferson employees were reported frequently in the news. In November 1908, Joseph Bryan, principal owner since 1905, died of heart failure at Laburnum, his country residence. John S. Mosby served as one of the honorary pallbearers.

Peter Fry, longtime Jefferson Hotel man and manager since 1897, resigned at the end of 1909 for health concerns. A couple months earlier, it had been reported he was unable to take charge of hotel business because of failing health. But he was quickly talked out of retirement to work at the White Sulphur Springs Resort in West Virginia. He didn't work there much longer, however, as he died in 1911. In January 1910, assistant manager Oscar F. Weisiger moved up to the manager spot.

An interesting story of The Jefferson concerned Robert Bauer, an employee of the hotel's Turkish baths. In September 1909, Bauer received the Carnegie Hero Fund Award (which came with $1,000 in gold) for his courageous efforts in trying to save Edward Barnes from drowning in the James River.

"A hapless, gaping crowd stood on the bank and groaned at the horror of it," the story related. Barnes had been boating with friends during a storm. To show their appreciation, a vaudeville act by the name of Allen & Jones did a benefit show for Bauer. Tickets to see Sam Allen and Russell Jones ("the man with a carpet bag full of funny things") were ten cents for children and fifteen cents for adults. A full five months after the incident, Bauer was reported to have been ill since the rescue attempt and was still at home recovering. Bauer told the press he wanted to get out of the hotel business and buy a place large enough to raise thoroughbred chickens. Apparently, the deceased Barnes (and a man named Jones) had been claiming squatter's rights on a very small island (described as nearly valueless) in the James River. They built a clubhouse on the island.

A woman named Mrs. Alfred E. Dieterich made the headlines in a big way and in a manner no one wanted. Not a hotel employee, she was more like family. Lewis Ginter had a nephew and three nieces—Grace, Joanna and Minnie Arents. An epic scandal involving Minnie's daughter, Mrs. Alfred E. Dieterich (née Edna H. Young), rocked Richmond and the country in September 1907, when this twenty-seven-year-old wife of a Standard Oil executive "whose wealth runs in the millions," ran off—or sailed off, to be more precise—to Paris with Harry Brenchley, her coachman. Before her marriage to Dieterich, she was a society girl in Richmond. Edna and Albert Dieterich had a five-year-old daughter named Grace.

Years earlier, Edna Young had been first mentioned in the Richmond papers in April 1897 for arranging a dance for the Lenton Sewing Club, a group of girls who got together every Monday during Lent to sew clothes for the children of the Day Nursery and Free Kindergarten. She later showed up in November 1900 for hosting the Westbrook Cup, named for her mother's country home. At a New York horse show, her chestnut gelding Buck won the $150 first place prize.

She met Brenchley through horses; that is, she paid him to train and show her horses. They traveled to Europe under a fictitious married couple's name. Running off to Europe with a coachman and leaving behind a young daughter and millionaire husband was not just a scandal, it was a family tragedy. Papers across America plastered this scandal on front pages. Ginter family friend Anton Thierman stepped in with an offer to help get Edna back home. The details of his offer are unknown, but here is Grace Arents's reply:

> *Dear Tony, I have just had a letter from Mrs. Young in which she says you have written to her and to Lewis asking for Edna's address, and offering to go to her if desired. Mrs. Young is not able to write about Edna to anyone and she asked me to tell you for herself and Lewis that she appreciates your affection for Edna but you can hardly suppose there is anything you could do that her mother and brother have left undone. As for what you suggest—that is impossible. I told you how useless we regard such an action, and Mrs. Young could never let Lewis do anything that would risk the life of the only child she has left—as for you making a personal matter of it, you have your own wife and children to consider. Time is the only helper now for this great sorrow. The only address we have, I gave you—c/o Tho[ma]s Cook, Paris. Thanking you again for all your sympathy and interest.*

In March 1908, it was reported that the couple would return from Paris to New York within a few days to "face the music." The next month in New York, Alfred Dieterich got a divorce and custody of Grace.

Various crimes against the hotel occurred. Former Jefferson Orchestra director Henry Z. Rees mysteriously disappeared, and the papers took note, reporting that his financial affairs were "in bad shape." After cutting ties with The Jefferson in April 1908, Rees moved to Laurens, South Carolina. It was alleged that he was taking hack fare from Jefferson Hotel guests and not turning the money over to the hotel. The article reported that Rees cashed a check in Atlanta and had not been seen for several days.

Detective Captain Tom Griffin had been hired by the hotel following approval by the Virginia legislature on March 9, 1900. A bill authorized The Jefferson Hotel Company to appoint a special policeman, with constabulary powers on hotel premises, to be paid by the hotel company: "Said police agent may cause any person so arrested by him to be detained and delivered to the proper authorities for trial as soon as practicable. Such police shall wear an appropriate badge."

Griffin was the subject of an odd story in August 1909 that claimed the lawman could predict upcoming rains based on recent full moons.

His name came up again in November 1909 when "fully 2/3 of all Richmond residents with phones" called the hotel asking about "certain terrestrial rumblings" from near the hotel. The hotel sent Griffin to investigate. This "rotund Sherlock" made his way to the Penitentiary Bottom area, where he learned it was a harmless steam machine.

There was no shortage of curiosities and con men, including W.H. Farnum, alias Dr. J.B. Weddell. From Troy, New York, Farnum was described as about thirty and having a good appearance. He claimed to be in the newspaper business and said he had gone south to Richmond for the warmer weather. On January 14, 1909, while basking in Richmond's warmer climes, he just happened to pass two bogus checks at The Jefferson in which he changed the amounts. The checks were for ten dollars (changed to fifty dollars) and five dollars (changed to fifteen dollars). Farnum was believed to have passed bogus checks in many states. A detective from Texas named A.T. Corwin arrived in Virginia to physically take Farnum back to face criminal charges in the Lone Star State. Corwin shackled Farnum's wrists and legs to prevent him from escaping. But Farnum had a long history of eluding the law, so much so that a newspaper story reported, "Down in Texas, they're betting heavily that Corwin will never bring his man in, knowing Farnum escaped once before."

While the Farnum caper was going on, a man named James G. Stickney, using the alias J. Elmer, passed a $375 worthless check at The Jefferson Hotel. It was accepted because he had the "appearance of being a man of good circumstances and his address was such that no question was asked." But they had their doubts. After Elmer checked out, hotel authorities telegrammed the South Dakota bank on which the check was drawn and found out four hours later that the check was "an out and out forgery." Richmond police chief Louis Werner sent telegrams to several East Coast cities providing a description of Elmer, as well as the woman traveling with him, a tall blonde wearing a green veil. The Jefferson also hired a Jersey City law firm to try to get its money back. On September 23, 1909, New Jersey authorities contacted The Jefferson. They had arrested Elmer, who had "excited no unusual interest" upon his arrival. While detectives of the New Jersey Central Railroad went through his baggage, Elmer shot and killed himself at a railroad station in Communipaw, New Jersey. They found $300.76 in his possession, which they sent to The Jefferson. The woman was not charged. On the same day that Elmer died, an innocent man was arrested in Norfolk, Virginia, in a case of mistaken identity because U.S. coastal authorities there thought he was the wanted man with the green-veiled woman. Of course, they had no way of knowing the real perpetrator was dead. It turns out that the man in Norfolk was near—but not with—a woman who happened to be wearing a green veil.

There was sad news, too. A seven-year-old girl died a few hours after attending a Valentine's Day party at the hotel in 1909. Josephine Woodward went to the party—to benefit the Home for the Incurables—and quickly got ill and died. It was reported that she had previously unidentified health problems. A girl referred to as Little Mabel Lomdey was much luckier. At The Jefferson 1903 Valentine's Day party, she wandered off from her mother and for several hours was lost. Eventually, she was found in the Capitol Square. The crying youngster was returned to her mother, who was reported to be the maid for Madame Herrmann.

Perhaps the most bizarre casualty was the accident causing the death of the fifty-five-year-old niece of General William T. Sherman. In April 1908, Lida W. Sherman Hoyt traveled from her home on Oyster Bay, Long Island, in New York to Richmond with her millionaire banker husband, Colgate Hoyt, to look at property to buy. They made the trip in a thirteen-foot, $10,000, sixty-five-horsepower French touring car, "one of the finest that has ever come into Richmond." Colgate Hoyt was president of the Automobile Club of America. During the trip, the "machine" got stuck for four hours in the mud and had to be pulled out by eight mules.

On April 28, 1908, Mrs. Hoyt "met a slight accident…just as she was leaving The Jefferson Hotel at the Main Street doors. She reached the door—a slight, frame affair, which swings back and forth—as a woman was preparing to enter. She was knocked down and somewhat bruised. She had to be lifted into a chair which was carried to her room." A physician was summoned and reported that she was not seriously hurt. But in fact, she was hurt very seriously. After the accident, she spent a month in her hotel room until she was taken by yacht to her New York home. Never recovering from the accident, she died on September 15, 1908.

THE '10S AND '20S

In December 1913, "the American Committee for the Celebration of the 100th Anniversary of Peace Among English Speaking People" convened at The Jefferson, blissfully having no way of knowing that the First World War was only a few months away. The Jefferson, like hotels around the country, did its part during the war. The *New York Times* reported in July 1917 that five national hotel men had been named to the National Hotel Committee on Food Conservation, an effort to conserve foods needed for the war. The Southern Region's representative was The Jefferson's own Charles Consolvo. The group agreed to do everything practicable to encourage hotels to cut down on certain foods from hotel restaurants.

"There is no class in the United States more patriotic," the story declared, "than the hotel men of America." There was, however, a suspicion that modern hotels, principally because of the dizzying array of choices on the average menu, operated "under a plan of superwastefulness." The fear that they might be called unpatriotic if they provided too much variety prompted the hotel men to switch to new "Hoover menus," named for Herbert Hoover, the future president and the man leading the national effort. To conserve, hotels would serve smaller "war portions." To save fats such as butter and lard, they would do less frying during food preparation. Wheat bread would be diluted by replacing 10 percent of the wheat with rye, corn or rice. Sugar was reduced across the board. To save meat, one day each week would be a "beefless day." It was not all bad news, however; they wouldn't skimp on foods not sent to Europe, like oysters, fish, lobsters, vegetables and fruits.

Hotel life continued as usual during and following the war years. Conventioneers convened. The Young Women's Christian Association got together to discuss matters, and in November 1915, the Southern States Women's Suffrage Conference held its convention. This was the decade of the suffragettes, so the hotel had its share of political discourse on the subject. In January 1910, Dr. Anna Howard Shaw, president of the National Suffrage Association, lectured at the hotel. She was as witty, according to the newspaper, "as the wind of the Northwest, and as delightful as the balsamic odors borne thereon." In 1909, a group of Richmond women, including the writer Ellen Glasgow, formed the Equal Suffrage League of Virginia. The Nineteenth Amendment, giving women the right to vote, passed in August 1920. To add a little levity to the topic, Miss Fola La Folette performed the English suffragist comedy *How the Vote Was Won.*

The Sons of the American Revolution got united for its annual conventions, and in June 1910, the Descendants of the Signers of the Declaration of Independence met. The United Daughters of the Confederacy got together at the hotel just about every year. Perhaps in 1912, the ladies saw the Great Seal of the Confederacy, a historic relic that had been buried in someone's attic for decades. After forty years of being "lost," the original seal turned up and was, at least as of June 21, 1912, in a locked hotel vault. Thomas Bryan, Eppa Hunton Jr. and William White, three prominent Virginians, purchased it for $3,000 from Thomas O. Selfridge, a retired U.S. Navy admiral. At the end of the Civil War, William Bromwell, a clerk in the Confederate States government, took the seal during the evacuation of Richmond. Seven years later, he sold it, along with various Confederate papers, to the U.S. government for $75,000. Selfridge was the government agent taking possession of the papers in Hamilton, Ontario. Somehow he ended up with the seal. Selfridge kept the seal at his house in Washington, D.C., from 1872 until 1912.

Regarding the War Between the States, a group (consisting primarily of New Yorkers) gathered at The Jefferson Hotel on April 27, 1914, to celebrate the birthday of Union general Ulysses Grant. They stopped in Richmond during a trip to Georgia for a dedication. The final report, a diary of sorts, prepared under the auspices of the State of New York, included:

> *We assemble to-day (in Richmond) with no malice toward the people of this section and they receive us with open arms. We come here with our hearts filled with love, kindness and devotion for all mankind and with the spirit of oneness and unity…Some wit of Richmond has announced in the morning papers that on the 92nd birthday of General Grant the Yankees have "entered Richmond, unannounced and unopposed." (Laughter and applause.) I regret that we were unannounced but am glad we were unopposed.*

The National Association of Postmasters delivered more than two thousand delegates to its thirteenth annual meeting in September 1910 with Polk Miller and His Old South Quartet stamping its own style of entertainment. The versatile Polk Miller came up again, in February 1912, when forty druggists from all over Virginia met at The Jefferson and formed the State Rexall Club, dedicated to procuring greater efficiency in the drug business. As honorary president, they elected Polk Miller, the pharmacist, the entertainer and the musician.

POLK MILLER

Polk Miller keeps poking up in the old stories related to Richmond and The Jefferson. In 1871, he opened a drugstore at 834 East Main Street. An ad from February 1900 shows the address of the Polk Miller Drug Company at 900 Main Street. He sold most of the typical remedies of the day. For twenty-five cents a gallon, he would deliver Bear Lithia Water. Polk Miller Drug had a successful mineral water and cigar department. Many household products were marketed as containing radium, including candy, facial cream, toothpaste, soaps, lotions and soda. And the amazing chemical cured almost everything, or so believers were led to believe, including malaria, tuberculosis, diphtheria, Hodgkin's, rheumatism, rabies, arthritis, epilepsy and even wife beating. It reversed the aging process and even helped pre-determine the gender of a baby.

But Miller's real claim to fame—and it's a big one—is still around and is now a multimillion-dollar (perhaps billion-dollar) corporation, and it's named for his dog: Sergeant. Miller was one of the first druggists to sell products for the health and well-being of dogs. A few decades later, you end up with Sergeant's Pet Products. As late as 1986, the company that became Sergeant's Pet Products was still referred to as the Polk Miller Products Corporation.

Miller's name surfaced prominently in the newspapers in the late 1890s and the first decade of the twentieth century, including on May 6, 1900, when the American Pharmaceutical Association held its forty-eighth annual convention at The Jefferson, with as many as five hundred attendees. The *Richmond Dispatch* carried drawings of Polk Miller and eight other prominent members of the organization. The program included "a run down to the Old Point," as well as entertainment by Polk Miller on The Jefferson Roof Garden.

Pharmacist Miller's real passion was entertaining. He led many musical shows, and his name was regularly mentioned in stories where one convention or another hired him to provide musical entertainment. Miller himself played the banjo. He didn't perform just in Richmond, either. He was all over. The Valentine Museum has Miller's scrapbooks, and in reading them, you feel challenged to try to keep up with his travels. His obituary in 1913 reported that he performed 3,000 shows in the last fifteen years of his life. The book *Men of Mark in Virginia* claims that Miller gave 2,500 performances from Maine to Texas.

He was at the YMCA in Washington, D.C., in April 1893, billed as "the banjoist, humorist and impersonator of old times in the South." He performed at Willard's Hall before heading back south to Williamsburg. A few months later, he was at Madison Square Garden, being introduced by Mark Twain as "the only original and utterly American thing" in the entire country. There were stops just about everywhere. In April 1895, he was touring through New Orleans to Huntsville, Alabama, and Nashville, before heading to Houston, Kansas City and St. Louis. Back in Washington, D.C., in January 1897, he was introduced by Senator Daniel as "the greatest one-man show on earth." The travels seemed endless: Baltimore's Lehmann Hall in January 1897; Westchester and Uniontown, Pennsylvania, a couple weeks later; Canton, Ohio; and then north and west to Kalamazoo and Detroit and Bloomington, topped off with a trip to the Northeast, where the stops included Syracuse, New York. Then he was in Raleigh and Wilmington. At all these places, he performed the banjo, played some music and made some jokes and wisecracks. He also regularly gave his famous "Old Times in the South" lecture. The simple headline in the *Nashville Banner* probably best summed up the headlines for all his shows: "Mirth Reigned Supreme."

But even Polk Miller's Pet Products couldn't have helped two women who had dog problems at the hotel in January 1911. What they needed was Peter Fry, the former manager who, against rules, had earlier let them keep their dogs with them overnight at the hotel. Fry's replacement, Oscar Weisiger, wasn't bending that rule, and his rigid conformity resulted in many national newspaper stories.

In the early part of January 1911, Mrs. James Brown Potter of New York—Richmond's own May Handy—was refused a room at The Jefferson because she brought her French poodle. Seven years after her marriage, the woman who had for years been regularly called "the most beautiful woman in Virginia" was referred to in Fredericksburg, Virginia's paper as "the former beauty." The hotel "interposed an objection...The incident was kept secret until ladies got hold of it. It has created a good deal of talk." The *New York Tribune* reported that both managers, Mr. Weisiger and Mr. Bigger, declined on the dog, but Fry would have allowed it. Mrs. Potter and her dog left the hotel and stayed at her sister's house instead.

Also in January 1911, an English actress named Olga Nethersole unsuccessfully tried to register with her dog. She had been involved in a controversial play called *Sappho*, which was frequently denounced as lascivious. One critic called it "a reeking compost of filth"; another claimed his morals "had been jarred." Miss Nethersole "needed to deodorize it [the play], and then burn it and forget it." In March 1900, she was indicted for "unlawfully, wickedly and scandalously" exhibiting material that "grievously offended public decency." The play's controversial scene was performed for the jury, with Nethersole and the actors in full stage costumes. After sixteen minutes, the jury voted not guilty.

T.A. MILLER

T.A. Miller, a competing pharmacist at the time, had a drugstore inside The Jefferson Hotel. In the newspaper drawing of nine prominent druggists attending The Jefferson convention, T.A. Miller was displayed in the center, with the others circled around him.

To generate buzz and attract customers, he offered at one point a raffle—held daily—where the winner would receive five dollars in gold. Any customer who spent at least twenty-five cents that day was entered in the raffle. Another marketing gimmick, in August 1903, involved a raffle where the customer holding the winning ticket, which was picked at the end of the month, got a complete refund of his entire purchase.

One advertisement claimed that he sold 320 dozen "Miller Malts" in the first seven months of 1898. For fifteen cents a bottle, Miller Malts promised to "restore your appetite, help you digest your food, make you sleep, strengthen your nerves and build up your system generally." He sold the usual tonics and remedies of the day: Paine's Celery Compound, Gude's Pepto Mangans and Carter's Liver Pills. What customer could go without Celery Phosphate, "the new drink—refreshing and appetizing!" or something for colds called

"Meyer's Kil-Kold tablets"? The tablets—get your billfold out—also "cured grip, headache and malaria, too."

Back to hotel conventions, where horse folks rode together under the aegis of the Guernsey Breeders Association, which saddled up in October 1915. People tied together by cotton met at that group's fifteenth annual gathering in May 1911. Smokers puffed away at the Tobacco Association's annual convention, and about two thousand delegates of the Laundrymen's National Association were pressed together in October 1910 for their twenty-seventh annual convention. Delegates marveled at exhibits of "everything from automatic wringing machines to soap that will float...one man asserts he has a machine which will press collars without breaking them in the fold." Members of the American Gas Institute were warmly greeted by Governor Mann and Mayor Ainslie.

Owners of baseball teams in the Virginia League hit The Jefferson in March 1912 and batted around some numbers related to averages and statistics. A story entitled "Base Ball Dope" reported their disagreements about splitting up the revenue. A couple years earlier, Charles Ebbets, president of the Brooklyn Dodgers of the National League, stayed at The Jefferson.

And what list of meetings can leave out politicians? In August 1912, the Conference of Governors meeting was held at The Jefferson. One curious item culled from the old newspapers relates to a recommendation by Connecticut governor Simeon Baldwin, who advocated a whipping post for wife-beaters. He claimed monetary fines weren't doing much good, but "bodily punishment" would "discourage wife-beaters better than anything else."

Even an organization called the Wednesday Club met. Established "to encourage musical culture in the City of Richmond," this group orchestrated its twenty-eighth annual music festival at the end of the decade. One of its leaders suggested that businessmen donate $50 to $100 each so the group could establish a chorus and "bring splendid orchestras and the most noted singers to Richmond," a city he claimed was "far behind other cities of its size in the South in respect to music."

In February 1912, the Richmond Chamber of Commerce held a smoker, the idea being to get people talking about building the one-hundred-mile link of the Quebec–Miami highway from Washington to Richmond. Not to be overlooked, the American Automobile Association had its annual meeting. Cars were just coming on the scene, and building roads to accommodate them was the talk of the day. In September 1910, The Jefferson ran an advertisement under the caption "Special Dining Room for Automobile Parties." Perhaps the Fraternal Order of Eagles saw the notice. Members made a point to stop at The Jefferson on their trip from New York to Columbia, South Carolina.

Cars were extremely dangerous, even then. In October 1912, an automobile carrying six women ran into a tree at Fourth and Grace Streets. One of the ladies "was thrown from the machine" and sustained a severe cut on her forehead. Stitches were sewn, and she recovered back in her room at The Jefferson, where she was staying while her husband attended a conference. Accident by automobile was a real possibility at that time. John Carrere, one of the hotel's architects, died in March 1911 from an accident near his home in New York City. He got hit by a taxicab just as he was getting into another taxi. He had been set to sail for Europe the day after the accident. A few years later, Richmond architect Carl Ruehrmund was hit and severely injured by a car at West Broad and Meadow. The Richmond Automobile Association offered $100 for the arrest and conviction of the driver, and the police department promised an extra week's vacation to the officer who found the culprit.

Believe it or not, some people worried about gas mileage even back then; at least, an inventor named J.A. Stransky of Pukwana, South Dakota, did. In going through a cache of Jefferson documents, I found a letter in which Mr. Stransky claimed that the U.S. government had determined that 30 to 50 percent of all gasoline was wasted on poor mixtures. Mr. Stransky determined that this problem alone wasted more than 1 million gallons of gasoline a day or about 400 million a year. The value of those 400 million gallons, according to the letter, was about $100 million, which works out to about twenty-five cents a gallon. It's not clear how Mr. Stransky's letter ended up in the trove of hotel documents. Perhaps he tried to sell his invention, the "Vaporizer," at one of the automobile-related conferences. According to the letter, the Vaporizer increased gas mileage by about 40 percent, from 21.2 miles per gallon to 29.6 miles per gallon, leading to this concluding sales pitch: "Why don't you try the Stransky Vaporizer and show yourself that YOU can have a motor that runs as smoothly as a fine watch, and entirely free from carbon trouble?"

The Richmond Chamber of Commerce met again in 1915, this time joined by 126 representatives from all counties of Virginia, to form the Virginia branch of the Southern Settlement and Development Organization. The goal: to finalize plans for bringing desirable settlers into Virginia. The state's population at the time was a little more than two million. The city of Richmond's population doubled from 85,050 to 171,667 in the period from 1900 to 1920.

People from all over the East Coast knew about the hotel, including George Vanderbilt of Princeton, New Jersey, a former United States senator who in retirement wrote about his travels through the South. In a story from 1915 entitled "Down in Old Virginia," he proclaimed The Jefferson Hotel "equal in its appointments of any modern hotel to be found in our country." But he didn't mention the alligators.

Edith (last name unknown), an anonymous author, sent home a letter at about the same time, telling her "dear papa" about the hotel. She said she thought herself very clever for figuring out how to get to The Jefferson by trolley. "This hotel," she gushed,

> *is a wonder, in fact they say it is well known all over the country and I can readily believe it. There is a beautiful statue of Jefferson in the court of the palm room, inside the hotel and the whole place is wonderfully furnished.*

Edith didn't mention the alligators, either. Senator Vanderbilt and anonymous Edith knew about the hotel's fine qualities, but not its finances. But you will:

Year	Assets/ Liabilities	Net Profits	Dividends	Repairs/ Maintenance
1910	1,595,066.07	95,593.27	31,580	16,030.45
1911	1,613,292.59	100,259.29	62,470	16,961.80
1912	1,805,782.26	102,877.04	97,000	25,429.72
1913	1,782,458.21	94,305.99	85,750	32,388.41
1914	1,749,840.38	73,287.78	61,000	23,574.07
1915	1,751,296.16	49,547.79	43,000	unknown
1916	1,741,905.14	68,586.60	73,000	30,691.95
1917	1,739,003.53	53,090.70	49,000	21,477.54
1918	1,773,411.85	88,547.99	79,000	24,226.26
1919	1,843,126.95	79,818.29	43,000	34,749.15

The 1913 expense for repairs and maintenance included the installation of a new roof, new boiler tubes, new carpets and a new skylight for the Franklin Street dome. As of November 1910, real estate taxes indicated that The Jefferson was valued at $497,850. Murphy's, at $413,726, came in as the next most valuable Richmond hotel.

ENTERTAINMENT

One of the most entertaining events of the era was the February 29, 1916 meeting of the Ladies' Night of the Richmond Rotary Club, when the ladies held their third annual convention adorned with the slogan: "Yes—Richmond is a Good Town." They toasted, "Here's to the friends we class as old / and here's to those we class as new. / May the new grow to us old / And the old ne'er grow to us new." Len Garvey's Orchestra provided the entertainment—the song sheet included the "Rotary Club Song," "There's a Girl in Havana" and everyone's favorite to wrap things up at the end of a long evening, "Auld Lang Syne." The program allowed thirty minutes for a session called "Wit and Wisdom," another thirty for "Music and Man Talk" and an unspecified amount of time for the ladies' real treat: an auction of single men.

And there was more. People danced, and prizes were awarded. The prizes included a barrel of apples donated by F.L. Butler and Honey Fruit Chewing Gum from Richard Gwathmey. Mrs. E.G. Kidd provided five one-gallon kits of Pin-Money Pickles; M.B. Florsheim threw in ten one-dollar laundry tickets; Robert Kaehler of Kaehler Motor Company donated five auto robes; the Corley Company gave six Victrolas; and the West Virginia Coal Company unloaded one ton of coal.

It's unknown whether the ladies drank much alcohol that night in February 1916, but perhaps they should have because soon after they wouldn't be able to get a drink at all. While the war raged in Europe, arguments over alcohol here in America got serious. National Prohibition went into effect on January 17, 1920 (Virginia was the second state to ratify the Eighteenth Amendment, which outlawed liquor), but many states had legislated anti-drinking ordinances several years earlier. In fact, at the time of the 1916 presidential election, twenty-three of the forty-eight states were "dry." Acquisition and consumption of alcohol by Virginia residents were significantly curtailed as of November 1, 1916, the day the Mapp Act went into effect. Named for George Walter Mapp, the ordinance had passed in a statewide vote of 94,251 to 63,886. Another big anti-drinking force at the time was Governor William Hodges Mann, who served from February 1910 to February 1914. According to *The History of Virginia*:

> *No satisfactory account of prohibition and temperance in Virginia should be written without giving Judge Mann a most responsible role. He was a pioneer in that cause when prohibition was a matter of ridicule with most people...The service which above all others distinguished him was in introducing and having passed what was known as the Mann Bill, which closed about 800 saloons in the country districts where there was no police protection.*

Alcohol purchased before the act and alcohol purchased outside the state were legal. People were allowed to "import" one quart of liquor and three gallons of beer or one gallon of wine each month, hence giving the act its nickname: the "one-quart law." The *Bluefield* [Virginia] *Daily Telegraph* reported that hotels in Virginia had pushed for, and received, an exemption from the Mapp Prohibition Law:

> *The big hotels of Richmond are said to have put up a fight for this purpose, stating that many of the guests enjoyed being rubbed down with booze as well as liking it in their victuals...The hotel proprietor is supposed to deliver in person the booze to his guest when the said guest makes it known that he is about to retire and is taking his bath and calls that he is ready for the rub-down. The fashionable Jefferson Hotel is said to have been among the hotels asking for this concession.*

Revealing that automobiles were still competing against horses as the principal mode of transportation, consider that one of the first conventions of the 1920s was the Carriage Builders National Association. A few years earlier, the International Blacksmiths Association forged its twenty-first annual convention at the hotel.

On November 23, 1921, French World War I leader Ferdinand Foch was honored at a hotel dinner. In charge of all allied armies during the Great War, it was estimated that he commanded ten million soldiers. Described by one historian as having "the most original and subtle mind of the French army," Foch is credited with bringing about "the intellectual and moral regeneration of the French Army." One thing he certainly brought were poetic quotes that make him seem like France's Will Rodgers. He talked about how the will to conquer was the first condition of victory and that the most powerful weapon on earth was "the human soul of fire." This poet in uniform also sprung this gem, which applies to anyone, anywhere: "In whatever you find yourself, determine first your objective."

In his introductory comments, toastmaster Eppa Hunton shared a well-known remark uttered by Foch at the bleakest of periods for the French during the war, when it appeared the Germans might soon be toasting tall glasses of white wine in Paris cafés: "My center is giving way, my right arm is falling back, I am giving the order to attack." To dramatize the solemnity of the event at the hotel, a pair of white doves, symbolizing "Peace," were set loose over the heads of the 394 guests at their preassigned seats at forty-eight tables.

Foch had let it be known he'd like to see the famous southern dance the "Virginia Reel," and that's exactly what he saw during the spiffy after-dinner ball at the Blues Armory. Spruced up in elaborate "rare lace and brocade, some of the lovely dresses belonging to grandmothers, and long laid away," and men "impressive in satin knee breeches and ruffled shirts," the specially trained cadre of twenty-four dancers reeled away the hours until nine o'clock, when the general and his entourage "with emotional farewells…showing little sign of fatigue" marched to the train that would take them to New York.

In the *Richmond Quarterly*, Eda Carter Williams described what happened next:

> *The late Mr. Frederick Satterfield (one of the "dancing bachelors") shortly before his death gave an amusing account of the end of that famous evening. Elated by their successful performance at the armory, the dance group had no intention of retiring at nine o'clock! Still in their costumes, they decided to proceed up to The Jefferson Hotel for late refreshment. On entering the lobby, they were introduced to a pair of irate British aristocrats, the Duke and Duchess of Sandwich, and they were much impressed. The Duke explained his anger to their willing ears: he and his wife had received a special invitation to the ball, but arriving late at the armory, they were turned away at the door! The explanation, which they did not accept, was that the crowd was so great there was fear the floor would collapse! With no*

urging, the group immediately offered to perform the "Reel" then and there, in honor of the Duke and Duchess of Sandwich. A musician was summoned to the lobby, and the dancers went through their paces for the second time. They were applauded with delight by the mollified British couple, who shook hands with each one.

The Jefferson Hotel suffered a few deaths in the family. James H. Dooley, one of the principal owners, died in November 1922, and Oscar F. Weisiger, longtime hotel employee and manager since 1911, passed away in 1927.

The American Chemical Society got its elements together for a seventy-third convention in April 1927. That same month, the Women's Club hosted its annual Easter Dance, with music by the Old Dominion Orchestra; the Junior League of Richmond held an event called "The Pirate Ball," its first moneymaking venture; and in December 1927, Richmonders of Italian descent hosted a reception for the Italian ambassador.

The highlight of 1927 flew in on October 15, when Charles Lindbergh landed at the hotel to be honored at a special dinner. Five months earlier, he became the first person to fly from New York to Paris. Skill, courage, four sandwiches, two canteens of water and 451 gallons of gas fueled the thirty-three-and-a-half-hour, 3,635-mile flight. The hotel's museum has a program from that auspicious gathering. Speakers included Governor Harry Byrd, Senator Claude Swanson, Congressman Andrew Montague and Douglas Freeman, editor of the *Richmond News Leader*. The Club-Southern Orchestra, directed by Frank Wendt, and the Southern Melodies Sabbath Glee Club, under the direction of Joseph Matthews, provided dinner music. In 1994, Gertrude Howland wrote to the hotel describing how her then eleven-year-old brother (Tommy Murrell Jr.) crawled under the table and sat at the feet of Lindbergh and Governor Byrd through the entire event. Earlier, Governor Byrd told Murrell to "stick around" and Byrd would arrange for him to meet Lindbergh. In making the famous flight, Lucky Lindy won a $25,000 prize.

To get an idea what a dollar was worth, let alone twenty-five thousand of them, consider that a menu from that period shows you could buy jumbo squab (broiled or roasted) or a Lobster Thermidor for $2.25. Sixty cents would get you a bowl of clear green turtle soup, grilled sardines on toast or a Smithfield ham sandwich. A caviar sandwich, a lobster salad or a Yorkshire Buck each cost $0.75. Budweiser beer was $0.35, a nickel less

Lindbergh Program, five months after the famous flight. *Courtesy of The Jefferson Hotel.*

than a milkshake with egg. The lunch menu reveals Pin-Money pickles were $0.25.

Here are some figures from the hotel's balance sheets from the 1920s:

Year	Assets/ Liabilities	Gross Profits	Net Profits	Dividends	Maintenance
1920	1,844,700.13	unknown	91,491.51	73,000	49,839.61
1921	1,900,323.33	465,853.84	60,178.63	unknown	44,945.07
1922	1,960,521.49	455,000.68	77,634.69	unknown	64,959.91
1923	2,117,502.19	509,662.68	118,331.39	unknown	63,581.95
1924	2,187,219.73	514,632.44	122,949.28	61,000	67,827.32
1925	2,258,286.21	521,270.80	117,771.99	61,000	34,501.00
1926	2,126,967.57	531,101.56	81,058.37	unknown	unknown
1927	2,116,508.70	564,551.48	78,750.42	61,000	46,948.71
1928	unknown	652,982.15	78,392.10	61,000	unknown

In November 1919, a company quoted the hotel the grand total of $570 to apply a coat of shellac and wax on the oak floors in the main dining room, men's room, passage and private dining room. Charles Consolvo signed the 1920 board report. As of February 1921, he owned 5,874 shares of the second preferred stock and 5,894 shares of common stock. Hotel Manager Weisiger owned 69 and 66 shares of each, respectively. John T. Wilson, the local contractor, was elected chairman of The Jefferson Hotel Corporation in 1923.

IV

The Depression Hits

We're in the late 1920s now, but let's momentarily skip ahead a bit and metaphorically flip the pages to get a glimpse of the hotel a half century into the future. The year is 1980. The hotel shuts downs and closes its doors. It stays closed for six long years. Three distinct factors led to that sad day, two of which happened almost simultaneously in October 1929: the Depression and the John Marshall Hotel. Starting in October 1929, the Depression and the John Marshall Hotel conspired to starve The Jefferson of revenue it critically needed for years to come. The Depression inflicted suffering everywhere and to everything, leading to massive cuts in discretionary spending, and hotels top any list of discretionary expenditures. But if the financial crisis were the only problem, the hotel might have recovered. After all, people—albeit fewer of them—still traveled to Richmond and needed nice hotel rooms.

To The Jefferson's great misfortune, however, a nicer, newer hotel opened in Richmond, almost on the very day the economy plummeted, pulling many of the remaining potential guests eastward, just a mile down Main Street. Suddenly, the John Marshall got the favorable superlatives, and the inauspicious description leftover for the thirty-four-year-old Jefferson Hotel was simply "old," a pernicious adjective for any high-end business and a veritable death sentence for a hotel. Money, a fabulous sum of money, was the only thing that could erase the nasty word: new renovations, new decor, new whatever to cover the haggard building. But starting in October 1929 and going well into the future, the John Marshall would grab much of the hotel revenue The Jefferson used to attract. The few remaining business travelers and thick-walleted, fresh-faced tourists no longer set their crisp twenties on The Jefferson registration desk or slid them into the hands of its hotel waiters. Instead, all those hundreds of thousands of dollars—big, fat, gaudy zeros—The Jefferson might have snared by renting basic rooms and gilded bridal suites, by serving juicy porterhouses and glistening Lobster Thermidors, by hosting corporate conventions or even just selling newspapers, ended up in the John Marshall bank account, oxygen-like dollars the wheezing Jefferson desperately needed for current and future renovations. Like an old boxer who's lost his zip, The Jefferson was walloped by the Depression and the John Marshall with a vicious one-two punch. The old warhorse stoically got back up and stolidly shuffled on but never recovered. This wicked October 1929 combination set up our hapless fighter for the final blow five decades later.

There's something appropriate about John Marshall being the name of the hotel causing so much economic harm to a hotel named for Thomas Jefferson. One hundred years before these two competing businesses reached skyward, the two legends of American history with the same names, two of Virginia's favorite sons—distant cousins by blood—waged a gentleman's political war against each other, unfailingly cordial and pleasant but never overcoming vast philosophical differences. It might have been more appropriate that the Marshall Hotel prevailed because John Marshall, a chief justice of the Supreme Court, actually lived in Richmond and called it home. His former Richmond residence is now a museum, next to the courthouse named for him. Thomas Jefferson, on the other hand, lived outside Charlottesville. He spent time in Richmond when he was governor. Phoenix-like, however, The Jefferson eventually does prevail—but all that comes much later.

Back to the long, slow decline of the 1930s, where the Depression still lurks, the haughty John Marshall gloats and The Jefferson gets hit with the another devastating punch: liquor, which for you numbers guys keeping score is the third factor. But the ray—nay, the scintilla— of financial sunshine from liquor gets smothered behind a cloud called Prohibition. Providing a hint of hope in the early years of the Depression, the fast current of liquor revenue streamed into hotel coffers, flowing in routes carved out by speakeasies everywhere. Sure, it was illegal, but The Jefferson flew under the radar, like all the others bootlegging during Prohibition. Happily snapping up some of the rare dollars still floating around in the 1930s, The Jefferson understood, like anyone who has ever done the math of mixed drinks understands, that liquor equals huge profits. Not enough profits for massive renovations, perhaps, but enough to keep things going. Profits during the Depression were a precious thing indeed, one to be protected from everyone and everything, including law enforcement officers. But on August 10, 1930, police officers busted into the hotel. When they later marched out with two five-gallon kegs of whiskey, twenty-six quarts and forty-one pints of liquor, they effectively turned this revenue stream into a stagnant dam. In referring to The Jefferson as a "Noted Hostelry," the *New York Times* reported that authorities seized liquor "popular in pre-prohibition days" and, for good measure, arrested, for storing ardent spirits, several hotel employees, including assistant manager Norman Whitman and head porter Frank Davis. Whitman and Davis denied knowledge of the liquor, and if there was any of it, they insisted, it belonged to the guests. Three days later, the charges against Whitman were dismissed for lack of evidence, but the cases against "several minor employees" were continued.

Once Prohibition finally ended in 1934, you might think The Jefferson would have started rolling in all that liquor revenue it missed during those dry years. Wrong. Remarkably, for an additional thirty-four more years after Prohibition was repealed, public establishments in Virginia—hotels and restaurants—were forbidden by law from serving mixed drinks. You read that last sentence right. An anti-drinking ordinance kept its death grip on The Jefferson, as well as every hotel in Virginia, until 1968. For all those decades before 1968, the notion that liquor might someday provide a legal source of lucrative revenue was a remote fantasy, like a man on the moon, which, as things turned out, ended up happening at about the same time. Little could they have imagined that, finally, decades later, when a law would finally pass legalizing liquor, a guy named Buzz would be skipping on the lunar surface a quarter million miles away.

Here's where the nasty little sucker punch otherwise known as liquor gets really bizarre. Not being allowed to sell alcohol all those years (until 1968) hurt the hotel's bottom line because it missed all that liquor revenue; surprisingly, the law making alcohol legal also hurt the hotel's bottom line, but in a way no one could have anticipated. Once the law finally passed legalizing liquor sales in 1968, you might think The Jefferson would have started rolling in liquor revenue. Wrong.

The anti-drinking ordinance caused several private clubs to open and operate in The Jefferson in the 1940s and 1950s, clubs where people could legally keep their own bottles of whiskey in private lockers and have cocktails with friends or business associates in comfort and style. This arrangement provided the hotel with steady monthly rental income for many years, and best of all, it was low-maintenance income. That is, to continue receiving the lucrative rental income from the clubs, the hotel did not have to do any advertising or any major renovations—or, in fact, much of anything. Once the clubs signed the lease and moved in, inertia kept them there. The Jefferson's owners loved the arrangement because the clubs weren't fickle overnight travelers looking for the best or the newest or whatever else overnight guests consider in deciding where to stay. The clubs were already there, at the hotel. And short of something extraordinary, they'd be there for good. Club members didn't really care if hotel operations were kept up or major renovations done. After all, they just wanted a place to relax, have a drink and then go home or back to the office. The revenue from these clubs allowed hotel owners to ignore major renovations. This simple strategy was ideal for all parties. The hotel couldn't afford renovations, and the clubs didn't care enough about them to pack up and leave. But this business model of cheating on renovations works only as long as the clubs stay at the hotel and keep paying rent, a prospect that seemed from the late 1940s until the mid-1960s as certain as Sinatra selling out the Mosque.

The 1968 law killed the clubs. Once bars or restaurants could serve liquor, why pay money to a private club and drive downtown to have a drink in an old hotel when you could stop at a place near your house or office? Sure, some clubs outside the hotel, like the Commonwealth, stayed in business. But one by one, in short order, the clubs renting space in the hotel held their auctions, sold their chairs and silver and sent the farewell-dear-member letters, actions that resulted in a giant sucking sound—that of future club revenue leaving The Jefferson Hotel's bank account.

Throw this below-the-belt, cheap-shot conundrum—lose without liquor, lose with it—at our old pugilist, and the future gets even blurrier. In slow motion, you see the final punch coming, can almost hear the arm swooshing through the air, pounding the beleaguered champ to the mat again, but this time when the referee calls out the final count, it's September 1980, and The Jefferson is a condemned, boarded-up building that used to be a grand hotel.

Now back to the Depression. Liquor prices were not recorded, but to get an idea of food prices at the time, menus from 1929 and 1930 show that dinner cost $2.50.

The board of director annual reports noted how the Depression negatively impacted business. Surprisingly, however, 1929 was a great year for the hotel. Even with the terrible last two months, gross profits of $655,484.54 and pre-depreciation net income of $126,343.20 were both record highs.

By 1930, gross profits dropped to $469,035.98, and pre-depreciation profits to $68,902.08, but the board congratulated itself for withstanding the economic disaster, noting, "It is rather gratifying, owing to the unusual depression, probably worse [sic] in the history of hotels in the way of business, that we have been able to make such a satisfactory showing."

In 1931, the directors again gave themselves high marks: "We have been able by economical operation and cutting our operating expenses to show an unusual profit under the circumstances...no institution in our industry has showed up quite as well." The number of directors was reduced from eight to seven. It had been increased from seven just a year earlier. Gross profits dropped again: to $354,041.14, with $28,800.87 in pre-depreciation income. After allowing for depreciation of $63,964.47, the hotel had a net loss of $35,163.60. Dividends were reduced, for a total paid of $25,000. Making matters worse, The Jefferson had lent money to the Monticello and the Belvedere Hotels. As of 1931, amidst this financial turmoil, The Jefferson was carrying accounts receivable from those two hotels of $39,750.00 and $40,198.98, respectively.

The 1932 report provided Charles Consolvo's brief summary of the history of The Jefferson from the time of his purchase of the second preferred and common stocks in 1921, at a time, according to Mr. Consolvo, when "the hotel was in bad repair and in a generally depleted condition, with no money in the treasury. Many thousands of dollars have been spent in improvements since then and...it is one of the best hotel properties of its class in the country." Consolvo opined that 90 percent of the hotels in the United States were in bankruptcy. The board was tightening its belt. Monthly payroll, for example, which cost $17,550 in December 1929, had been reduced to $5,802 for the month of October 1933. The board warned that the hotel code portion of the

Early postcard. *Courtesy of The Jefferson Hotel.*

newly enacted NRA (National Recovery Act) would probably cause payroll expenses to increase by 25 percent. The hotel corporation missed two consecutive monthly dividend payments in 1933, requiring an explanation to shareholders. Consolvo pleaded with shareholders to be patient, reminding them that "his life work and entire fortune" were invested in the hotel. He vowed "to cooperate and assist in any way…which might be desired by the preferred stockholders." The Jefferson was losing money but increased dividends to $36,500. Gross profits had dramatically declined from the prior year—to $235,611.12—and pre-depreciation profits were only $19,338.87. In addition to Consolvo, the directors, as of 1933, were Thomas B. Purcell, Preston B. Watt, O.H. Funsten, future governor James H. Price, John T. Wilson and John S. Bryan.

A 1936 report revealed that five separate loans totaling $48,000 to the Bank of Commerce and Trusts matured in 1936. As of June 30, 1936, the auditors valued The Jefferson at $1,508,836.79. For the first six months of 1936, the hotel generated a pre-depreciation profit of $33,735.54. After depreciation of $18,118.17, net profits for the six-month period were $15,617.37.

Sherrad Willcox Pollard, originator of the monodrama, which used elaborate costumes in each scene, premiered her new play *Symphony* for the Westhampton College Alumnae Association at The Jefferson Auditorium in November 1929. There were only two other women in America doing similar dramatic theater work. The Alumnae Association claimed it went to considerable expense to present Miss Pollard.

At a hotel award banquet in April 1931, Mary Lucile Saunders, a junior at Westhampton, won first place in a playwriting contest for her play, *The Son's Father*. The Richmond Academy of Arts and Crafts drew its First Arts and Crafts Tournament at The Jefferson in September 1931, and the National Bookbinders Association held its twelfth annual convention. A full-page advertisement proclaimed, "Where elegance and charm combine in a hotel of unexcelled comfort. Stop at The Jefferson in Richmond, Virginia—the city of romance and history—and enjoy the luxury of 'The Aristocrat of Southern Hotels.'"

Conventions, performances and exhibitions continued through the Depression. Thirty governors attended the National Governors' Conference in June 1932. Horace Gans, a longtime hotel resident, recalled sneaking in and assisting New York governor (and first-time presidential candidate) Franklin D. Roosevelt to a seat. Gans got in by marching with a governor from one of the Dakotas who did not have a military aid with him. FDR at that point walked with two canes, and Gans got him a chair so he could sit on the mezzanine. Each governor was announced to heralds and trumpets before descending the staircase. The loudest applause, according to the *Richmond News Leader*, went to FDR and to the Richmond-born governor of Maryland, Albert Ritchie.

The Beaux-Arts Ball, hosted by the Richmond Academy of the Arts, provided the entertainment. During the 1932 Beaux-Arts Festival, debutante Elinor Fry, honored as the "Spirit of Beaux-Arts," was lowered in something that was supposed to look like a tulip from the lobby skylight by a strand of piano wire before disappearing into a shower of balloons. Elinor Fry had a proud and noble lineage to The Jefferson Hotel. First, her father, Peter M. Fry, managed the hotel from 1897 until 1910. Second, and not many people in the hotel's history could say this, she was born (in 1903) in the hotel. Being up in the air was nothing new to her or her family. She might have had the distinction of being the first woman to be licensed as a pilot in Virginia. Her niece, Bettie Hobson, showed me the letter, dated September 17, 1929, from the Department of Commerce, Aeronautics Branch, authorizing Miss Fry to operate as a student pilot. Keep in mind that Lindbergh's 1927 flight across the Atlantic was less than two and a half years earlier. The form letter to Miss Fry came with a "Dear Sir" salutation, Sirs being the entire universe of potential recipients of that letter at the time. Someone at the Department of Commerce scratched out the Sir and replaced it with Madame. Tragedy, however, hit the flying Fry family in June 1931. Elinor's brother, known as "Skeeter," a thirty-two-year-old man about town who drove a Rolls-Royce convertible, was killed as he took off in an airplane from an airfield located near the Hill Monument on Laburnum. He was headed for a debutante party in Washington, D.C. After her brother's death, Elinor flew as a passenger in airplanes but never again piloted one.

ELINOR FRY

Someone ought to write a book about Elinor Fry. It's dizzying to read about everything she did. She played tennis and was an avid swimmer. She traveled. And she voraciously golfed and fenced. But her passion was dancing. For a while, the world was her stage—New York, Hollywood, Tokyo, Russia, Paris, Dresden and Mexico City. She had several offers to dance professionally, including one from Mr. Ziegfeld. She performed as the "Spirit of the Virgin Land" in the Virginia Historical Pageant in May 1922 and later played Jack Frost in the Arabian Nights Pageant. She loved teaching children, and to do so she opened a dance studio in 1920 at 2600 Monument Avenue. From there, she taught thousands over the decades—until May 1972, to be precise—including many blind and deaf children. Miss Fry would have made any short list of Richmonders who touched the most people in their lives. Each year her students—hundreds of them—performed at the Mosque. Mrs. Hobson's scrapbook contains many stories of the "Frylics," each followed with the year. The first show, the "Frylics of 1933," consisted of two hundred students. Helen Keller attended and "watched" the performance, according to a news account, by feeling vibrations from a tin cup in her hand. The shows from 1933 until 1941 were sponsored by the Virginia Association of Workers for the Blind. By the time the "Frylics of 1935" performed, there were three hundred children. Each year's show had a different theme, and all of the costumes for every show, every year, were hand-cut and handmade. Mrs. Hobson, who danced in a few of the shows as a little girl, proudly stated that there was not a single store-bought costume. Her scrapbook included the drawings of the incredibly creative costumes for each show. Some of the themes included: *Music of the First Half of the 20th Century*, *Famous Quotations and Familiar Phrases*, *Music the Whole World Loves* and even one in 1940 with a *Revue of Popular Cigarette Brands*. The "Frylics of 1962" performed dances to the theme of *Out of This World*, this being right after John Glenn flew to outer space. The program's cover that year featured a drawing of two children riding a rocket.

Elinor also put on many children's dance shows outside of the Frylics. The children performed shows to sell bonds during World War II. Once, in Civil War costumes, the Frylic Dancers marched like little soldiers down the stairs of The Jefferson Hotel and then performed a dance in the Rotunda.

Beaux-Arts Balls also took place at The Jefferson in 1931 and 1933. An unidentified Richmond news reporter came up with the idea of this entertainment event to lift the city "out of the slough of despond" during the Depression. In the 1931 ball, Miss Harriet Caperton rode in on a white charger, and 1933 ball-goers witnessed Miss Dorothy Mosby arrive in the Rotunda on a Sicilian cart drawn by a jackass. "He was a complete jackass," one story reported, "for he refused to move out of the spot light."

Richmond's own Bill "Bojangles" Robinson performed his dance steps at the 1932 ball. One of the legends about the hotel involves the celebrated Bojangles. His agent, Marty Forkin, concocted a story that Bojangles was plucked from obscurity while serving food at The Jefferson Hotel. Bojangles, the likely piece of fiction goes, spilled hot oyster stew on Forkin. The next day, Forkin happened to see the dancer performing on the street and signed him to a contract. Nice story and a good yarn, but who knows whether it's true?

In 1932, The Jefferson made national news, albeit in a minor way. After Mr. and Mrs. Charles Lindbergh's infant son was kidnapped from the Lindberghs' New Jersey home, a national dragnet ensued to find the baby and catch the kidnapper(s). People were glued to their newspapers and radios to hear the latest about the missing baby. Lindbergh and authorities looked everywhere, running down leads, including one that took them several miles out into the Atlantic Ocean. A forty-four-year-old shipbuilder named John Hughes Curtis convinced Lindbergh and authorities that he had been approached by a man who claimed to be in contact with the kidnappers. Curtis demanded the meetings take place at sea, several miles off the coast.

To assist, Jefferson Hotel primary owner Charles Consolvo lent his eighty-five-foot yacht, the *Marcon*. With Lindbergh; Mr. F.H. Lackman, the skipper of the yacht; Reverend Dean Harold Dobson-Peacock; retired Rear Admiral Guy Burrage; and Curtis aboard, the *Marcon* ended up making four mysterious trips to sea. All the newspapers reported the expeditions, albeit with maddeningly few details. Eventually, Lindbergh, thinking the *Marcon* had become too well known because of the press coverage, ended up using another ship for the clandestine meetings. Nothing came of these mysterious contacts. The baby was later found dead a few miles from the Lindberghs' home.

Curtis's shipbuilding business had been hit hard by the Depression, raising the obvious possibility that this was a wicked ruse to pick the pockets of the grief-stricken, desperate and very rich Lindbergh. In fact, as it turned out, Curtis was later convicted for his role in the extortion plot.

The Report of Hotel Operations by Horwath and Horwath, "Specialists in Hotel Accounting," compiled information from one hundred American hotels and calculated that, from 1932 to 1943, the lowest overnight charge was during February 1934, when rooms averaged $2.87. The lowest occupancy rate was June 1933, at 48.75 percent.

To celebrate the repeal of Prohibition in 1934, The Jefferson opened an indoor café. Looking like a Paris sidewalk café, the Terrace Room served beer and wine at the Franklin Street entrance. As previously mentioned, mixed drinks were still thirty-four years in the future.

There was a flurry of renovations. In August 1935, it was reported that the hotel would undergo $25,000 in redecoration work, expected to be completed within two months. Seven months later, an additional $50,000 for renovation and exterior cleaning work was to be done. Some of the ivy had to be sacrificed to clean the bricks, and modern electrical fixtures were installed. The story reported that some of the hotel's original $500 porcelain tubs were still in use. There were two newspaper stories about redecorating work on October 21, 1936; one reported the project cost $36,000, while the other had it at $75,000. It's not known whether these were separate projects or the reporters got their figures wrong.

Several paintings, which formerly hung in The Jefferson but were relegated to storage, came out of the basement and were put back up on the walls in 1936. In addition, a painting called *Une Fantasia au Moroc*, which had been sent years earlier to the Belvedere Hotel in Baltimore, came back to The Jefferson in 1936. Insured for the grand sum of $10,000, the painting must have been returned as part of Consolvo's termination with the Belvedere. All financial ties between Consolvo and the Belevedere were ended on February 14, 1936.

I found and reviewed a large volume of Belvedere records. The records listed an account receivable from The Jefferson Hotel (noted, along with the accounts receivable from the Monticello Hotel, as an affiliated concern) each year from 1921 to 1931 ranging from a low of $47.83 (in 1931) to a high of $10,055.90 (in 1926). The September 1935 Belvedere report mentioned that $164,182.25 of Jefferson Hotel stock had been written off, reducing the former amount to $492,746.75.

Helen Bertsch, an eighteen-year-old maid at Charles Consolvo's home, sued the Consolvos for $5,000 on September 24, 1930, for assault and defamation of character, claiming Mrs. Consolvo hit her. In May 1936, The Jefferson Realty Corporation sued Charles Tarjan, preventing him from using the name Jefferson Coffee Shop for his business at Adams and Main, a block from the hotel.

Right after Christmas 1936, Thomas Wolfe the writer (the first one) stopped at The Jefferson on his way to a writers' conference in North Carolina. By coincidence, the Modern Language Association (MLA) was holding its annual meeting in Richmond, with about 1,500 in attendance. What was initially an awkward accidental meeting turned out to be very enjoyable for Mr. Wolfe. He didn't personally care for many of the MLA writers but ended up getting along with them, sharing writing ideas and drinks.

The year 1940 had its share of historical footnotes. In January, Samuel James Tilden Moore Jr. published his fabulous book *The Jefferson Hotel: A Southern Landmark*. "This book, like The Jefferson," Mr. Moore wrote, "is dedicated to the exacting traveler." Mr. Moore articulated his fondness for the hotel:

> *All my life I have harbored a feeling of deep respect for The Jefferson Hotel and the spirit that it embodies. To me it is as much a part of Richmond as is Broad Street, the Capitol Square, or the James River. In fact, it would be hard to picture Richmond without "The Jefferson"...When the Yuletide season descends on this peaceful Southern city The Jefferson Hotel embellishes the largest Christmas*

tree that is available, decorated in a manner that is equally magnetic…When summer comes we Richmonders, hurrying along Franklin Street, slacken our pace when we pass The Jefferson…It is little wonder that I have found so much pleasure in writing about this unusual hotel. May it live forever. I know that its inexhaustible supply of pleasure will, for as Keats wrote, "A thing of beauty is a joy forever"…Since that Hallowe'en night of 1895 thousands of world dignitaries have passed through the portals of The Jefferson Hotel, yet each have paused on first entering the building and wondered how such an arrangement of beauty could have been born in the mind of one man.

An avid history buff, Moore portrayed Jefferson Davis, Thomas Jefferson, Robert E. Lee and George Washington in local reenactments and civic events. Moore also authored *Moore's Complete Civil War Guide to Richmond.* He served in World War II as a cryptologist in the Pacific Theatre and later worked as an attorney.

The Forty-first Session of the American Proctologic Society convened in June 1940, and a future United States president visited shortly afterward. Missouri senator Harry S Truman stayed at The Jefferson and wrote a letter to his wife, telling her he would have stayed longer if she had been with him, "but I got to thinking, well maybe there'll be a call from home or some other emergency I ought to know about; so I jumped in the car and came back." Truman added that he wished his wife could have seen The Jefferson Hotel:

It is built over a whole block, with a lobby all the way from street to street just like the old Baltimore was. There's a famous statue of Jefferson, a fish pond and a terrace dining room where I ate breakfast. Every hall is full of mirrors and it has two towers like a Spanish mission with a town clock in them. It is old but still high hat and very quiet and dignified.

Truman didn't mention the alligators. The Jefferson Hotel family suffered a loss in September 1941 when William C. Royer, the manager since 1935, passed away at age sixty-five of a heart attack. Even the *New York Times* ran an obituary of the "Southern Hotel Man for 40 years."

CONSOLVO BECOMES FULL OWNER

By February 16, 1943, when seventy-two year-old Colonel Charles Herbert Consolvo took over complete control of The Jefferson, he had already been a hotel baron for four decades. He got into the business in 1903, at a time when George Arents was still trying to decide whether to sell or rebuild The Jefferson after the 1901 fire. With his colorful background, Consolvo seems like the kind of guy everyone liked, the epitome of an old-time hotel man. He got along with high-profile celebrities, as well as common folks whose only mention in the news would be their obituary someday in the local paper. His office walls were covered with pictures of friends who were rich and famous and friends who were not. Consolvo was described in his obituary as a sparkling conversationalist who "presented his amazing stock of knowledge in many fields in an attractive manner," a comment that must have been true simply because it's so colorfully unique. Other newspapers reported he was a "humble man…courteous to a point."

This true-life Horatio Alger ran away from a foster home at age fifteen to join the circus and did not end up just selling peanuts. He performed as an acrobat, with reports indicating that he was pretty good at it, good enough to impress his friends for years afterward with his unique skills. He didn't stay in the circus very long, but it stayed with him. He attended hundreds of circuses for the rest of his life, forever maintaining friendships with circus folk, including owners and managers who always tried to frequent the hotel of their friend and former colleague. Consolvo's eighty-year-old grandson told me he vividly recalls his grandfather doing handstands for him in the mezzanine office of Norfolk's Monticello Hotel.

He started out by delivering things—newspapers, ice and coal—before eventually, in the 1890s, buying the Norfolk Steam Laundry with Edward Cheshire, his brother-in-law. To expand their business, they branched into advertising, and before long they owned almost all outdoor billboards in the Tidewater area. As of 1915, they operated twenty-five thousand linear feet of signs and billboards. Realizing the incoming bonanza and tourist dollars of hosting overflow visitors for the 1907 Jamestown Exposition, Consolvo took control of Norfolk's Monticello Hotel in 1903. It's not clear how he took control of it, but suffice it to say that it was a financial risk. Had it not been for the Jamestown Exposition, he later claimed, he would not have ended up in the hotel business. The Monticello gamble

paid off and made him lots of money, money he parleyed to acquire majority control of Richmond's Jefferson Hotel on October 27, 1920, and Baltimore's Belvedere Hotel in 1917.

Early in the century, he was a quartermaster general of the old Virginia Volunteers (the militia). Later, in 1913, he was appointed a "colonial" on the staff of his friend Minnesota governor Adolph Eberhardt and in so doing became the first and only out-of-state resident so honored. He served as a delegate to the 1932 Democrat National Convention.

Mentioned so often in the press in the 1920s, the newspapers might as well have carried a column called "Where's Mr. C?" with the winning prize a free stay at a Consolvo hotel. In June 1922, he was taking a train to Providence, Rhode Island, for the grand opening of the Biltmore Hotel; less than a year later, he was joining other nationally known hotel men in Buffalo, New York, for the opening of the Statler. June 1926 found him in New York City being honored with a prestigious award given by the French government. That was right after Consolvo and other prominent hotel men returned from a foreign working vacation. The *New York Times* reported in April 1926 that Consolvo and 350 other

The Consolvo Hotels. *Courtesy of Mary Stuart Cruickshank.*

hoteliers from thirty-five states and Canada would spend sixty-seven days in Europe visiting eight countries, where they "will be received by royalty in each." In March 1928, Consolvo and his wife were visiting Mr. and Mrs. John Ringling in Sarasota; the story had them arriving by boat, a fully accurate statement since an eighty-five-foot yacht is, by any definition, still a boat. Three days later, another report mentioned the fifty-seven-year-old Consolvo was so healthy and flexible that he could touch his toes, a feat, the story speculated, most likely possible because he took annual winter trips to Florida.

His first wife, Annie Cheshire, was the sister of his business partner, and his second wife, Blanche Hecht, was an opera singer. In July 1924, at the Hotel Ritz-Carlton in Atlantic City, Consolvo married his third and final wife, Mary Byrd, of the influential Byrd family of Virginia.

Three wives and the only offspring was a "mentally subnormal" adopted son named Charles Swanson Consolvo Jr. Physicians testified about his mental acuity during court proceedings when this heir to a fortune tried to get his marriage to a Baltimore beautician annulled. The *New York Times* described her as a pretty blonde. In September

1924, shortly after the wedding, she sued Colonel Charles Consolvo, her father-in-law, for $100,000 for alienation, claiming the colonel was preventing his son from living with her. This promptly led the colonel to try and buy Junior an annulment, arguing that Junior was drunk at the time of the wedding ceremony and mentally impaired all of the time. During the hearing, the young bride denied giving her husband the money to buy the ring and marriage license. A Howard County, Maryland judge agreed that nineteen-year-old Charles S. Consolvo was indeed mentally challenged but denied the annulment on the grounds that law trumps brains: "Young Consolvo may be stupid, but that does not relieve him from a contract." Three years later, on August 23, 1927, the man with the brains of a twelve-year-old shot and accidently wounded himself in the abdomen while cleaning his pistol.

Consolvo's only grandchild, Charles Consolvo III, heard rumors that his father (Charles Swanson Consolvo Jr.) was either adopted or the illegitimate son of Colonel Charles H. Consolvo. The topic was never discussed in the family.

According to *The Report of Hotel Operations*, the overall 1943 national occupancy rate was 89 percent, and the average room rate for December 1943 was $3.78.

Life during the war years continued at the hotel. In March 1943, Henry Taylor Wickham, president pro tempore of the Virginia Senate and part-time hotel resident, died in his winter home at The Jefferson at age ninety-three. Five elected officials represented the senate at his funeral; one of them was Aubrey Weaver, a very influential Virginia politician who would end up dying in a hotel fire about a year later.

THE FIRE OF 1944

It was Friday night, March 10, 1944. Nine engine companies, three truck companies, the reserve wagon and a foam wagon answered the call, getting the blaze under control in about an hour. There were about 425 guests in the hotel at the time, including many elected officials celebrating the closing of the legislative session and getting through some controversial legislation. Several people later claimed credit for notifying the hotel of the fire, including a state senator who learned of the fire by seeing, from his room, flames reflected on the building opposite the wing where he was located.

Wesley Vest, a bellhop, had been told by a soldier about the fire; together, they extinguished it—or at least thought they had. But like the 1901 fire, it continued out of sight. Vest claimed he told Mr. Hickman, the night clerk, about putting it out, but Hickman later insisted he never heard anything from the bellhop. The six dead were: Ruth Lyon Andrews of Durham, North Carolina, employed at the time at Bellwood; John Winston Ross, a ship's cook stationed at Camp Peary; Jean Manfredi, thirty-one, of Irvington, New Jersey; Dorothy Gann, forty, of Newark, New Jersey (Manfredi and Gann were found dead from suffocation in the bathroom of the room they were sharing: Room 601. They were in town to visit Miss Gann's brother, a Camp Peary sailor); Lillian Martin Price (she had moved into Room 600 of the hotel as a full-time resident in early 1944, shortly after the death of her husband, James Hubert Price, who served as governor of Virginia from 1938 to 1942; her son and friends identified her by her wedding ring); and Aubrey Gardner Weaver, sixty-two, affectionately known as "The Kingfish." (Weaver was celebrating with friends in Rooms 615–19. He had been a delegate to all Democrat National Conventions from 1928 to 1940, a member of the House of Delegates from 1912 to 1915 and a member of the senate from 1932 until his death. He became chairman of the State Finance Committee in 1940. "Ask Senator Weaver," one of the newspapers reported, "was an expression often heard in Capitol corridors when someone inquired about state finances…He could readily answer questions dealing with anything from the salary of a minor executive to estimated revenues of the Commonwealth for a two-year period." Weaver's wife was not at the party because she was in the hospital, about to give birth to a son.)

Originally, seven were reported dead. The next day, O. Clarence Green, a forty-three-year-old engineer, was "found," blissfully unaware that he was ever lost. The night of the fire, he told friends he was going to The Jefferson. Since his whereabouts after the fire were unknown, it was assumed he had perished.

Many hotel guests were injured by leaping from windows on the upper floors. At least one man let himself down from his window by tying bedclothes together. Those treated for injuries included: fireman Ralph Raffo, injured in a fall from the sixth to the fifth floor; Miss Maggie Dolan, a sixty-four year old housekeeper, burned on the feet;

John McMahon of Brooklyn, New York, overcome with smoke; and seventy-year-old Reverend John Scott in Room 587, burned on hands and feet. Scott and his sister had lived at the hotel since 1916. They moved out for good shortly after the fire. Delegate Edward DeJarnette (Room 682) was rescued by fireman A.H. Galbraith's heroic efforts to connect a twelve-foot "pompier" ladder to a fully outstretched eighty-five-foot ladder. Firemen rescued many people from their fourth-, fifth- and sixth-floor windows.

Miss Mary Ellis, the hotel operator, frantically called each room, telling people to get out. She later recalled that no one answered the phone in Senator Weaver's room. She also remembered receiving a couple of incoming calls from Room 601, pleading for help; a woman was screaming that she was smothering to death. Miss Ellis had only been on the job for less than four months.

Chaos and mayhem ruled the night, as described by Warrick Thompson, a *Richmond Times Dispatch* reporter who had been in Room 505. Undoubtedly, Thompson was at the hotel because of the politically connected entertaining going on. Thompson heard a ruckus about 11:45 p.m. but assumed armed forces members were having a loud party. He looked out and saw "a mass of flames" along the Adams Street wing. Thompson tried to call his paper to report the fire but couldn't get through to the operator. He opened the door to the hallway, "with no sense of impending danger," to be overwhelmed with "a dense, impenetrable mass of smoke." The hallway lights were out and the "horrifying screams of panicky people" inescapable. Soldiers made a beeline for fire hoses, and guests in varying degrees of clothing—wearing pajamas, with heavy overcoats and some with no shoes or socks—filled the staircase. After getting to the lobby and briefly calling the paper, Thompson went back up to his room to get his suitcase. The hotel elevator operator took him, saying he was crazy to want to go back. Back on the floor, the smoke had cleared somewhat, but Thompson could see flames in the hallway. He told the elevator operator to wait for him while he dashed into his room. Scurrying back to the elevator, he could see the operator's mouth moving, and Thompson knew the operator was screaming something, but he couldn't hear anything, like in one of those surreal movie scenes. The operator took him back to the lobby, where bodies were strewn about, covering the floor, including one man lying facedown with three civilians and several soldiers working on him. The throng screamed for a pulmotor. Ambulances had not yet arrived. The first physician on the scene, Dr. Fulmer Bright, cried, "My God, that's Senator Weaver, and I think he's done for!" People kept working on him until another doctor pronounced Weaver dead. Thompson heard the front desk operator comment, "My God, that's Room 601 calling again, pleading for help!" The caller claimed that she was trapped, and smoke was coming into the room. Dr. Bright exclaimed, "My God, I know almost everybody in this hotel…it is terrible, terrible, terrible!"

The police and firemen arrived, and the elevator operator took them up. Mayor Ambler claimed he had heard many strange things—the hoses were rotten, fire extinguishers didn't work, water pressure was too weak and the city fire hoses didn't fit onto the hotel fire plugs. He vowed to start an investigation before anything could be covered up. Thompson later saw volunteers working on two women laid out in the mezzanine. These were the New Jersey women trapped in Room 601.

The fire produced many heroes, principally the firemen and several members of the military. John Winston Ross, the sailor (ship's cook) who died, had insisted on staying and fighting the fire. A Lieutenant Milton Spilberg received recognition in the state legislature for saving eight-year-old Marthanne Stephens and her ten-year-old sister, Jean Stephens, from either Room 502 or 504, where their parents had left them while attending a party. The Stephenses had rented both rooms that night; there is no way to determine which room the girls were in. The newspapers reported that their parents were on the sixth floor with Senator Weaver's group, but both "girls" told me that their parents were at a party at the John Marshall Hotel. Before she was rescued, little Marthanne Stephens, according to a news account, tried calling the sixth floor looking for her parents, "but no one answered." Several friends and residents of the fifth floor had been asked to check in on the girls. One of those friends, a Mrs. Blanton, had a key, so she went to get the girls when the fire started. When she got near the room, she mistakenly thought she had left the key back in her room and didn't realize until much later that she had the key in her pocket all along. Thinking she didn't have the key, she went to find help and came up with Lieutenant Spilberg, who "waded through ankle-deep flames" to break down the door to save the girls. When commemorated, Spilberg "minimized his action in comparison to the brave efforts rendered by the other servicemen."

The Stephens girls: Jean Stephens Arrington (left) and Marthanne Stephens Smith. The sisters were rescued from the fire in 1944. *Courtesy of Jean Stephens Arrington and Marthanne Stephens Smith.*

Sixty-six years later, Jean Stephens Arrington and Marthanne Stephens Smith recalled waking up in their hotel room that tragic night and seeing smoke coming in from below the door. People were checking on them every hour until their parents returned. They had put the episode in the back of their minds and had never really talked about it. Although the girls were only ten and eight, they knew enough to keep the door closed and put a wet towel on the floor in front of the door. They also smartly covered their noses and mouths with wet towels. The sisters recalled remaining calm, and Marthanne remembers being most concerned during the fire about the new mink stole their mother had left in the closet of The Jefferson. They looked out their window and saw bedsheets from another window tied together to make a rope to climb down. They later heard that before or during their parents' mad rush back to The Jefferson, their mother fainted. Once the girls got down to the lobby, Jean remembers doing something she had never done before: drinking a cup of black coffee. A newspaper story ran a photo of Mrs. John Powell Williams and Red Cross volunteers serving coffee in the hotel that tragic night.

Delegate Delamater Davis, who was in Room 501, offered praise and thanks to an unidentified soldier and a British sailor who pounded on his door to alert him. Eleanor Durham observed a British sailor make five separate trips to the fifth or sixth floor, bringing a person down on the elevator with him on each trip.

In addition to heroes, the fire produced lawsuits, at least fifteen of them. The estates of Senator Weaver, Ruth Lyon Andrews, Dorothy Gann and Jean Manfredi each filed suit for $15,000. Senator Harry Stuart, hospitalized for about two weeks after the fire, sued for $7,500. Claimants had one year from the date of the fire to sue. On March 5, 1945, Jack Gansert, a professional New York dancer who claimed to be permanently injured from the fire, sued for $25,000. J. Eugene McMahon and Alfred Dellapenta, both of Buffalo, New York, and both in Room 689, each filed suit for $5,000. Also suing were hotel residents Reverend John G. Scott and his sister (one account reported her name as Mrs. Emma Scott Taylor, another as Mrs. J. Fenton Taylor). Even The Jefferson's dearest, oldest and longest-ever resident—Horace Gans, who was in Room 536—filed suit for $7,500. In a *Virginia-Pilot* story forty-two years later, Gans recalled:

I woke up from the noise of engines and confusion outside. There were no fire bells, no calls from the office downstairs or help. The hoses on the walls were too rotten to handle the water pressure. It was around midnight. Sparks were falling down past my window and the room was full of smoke. I threw a wet towel over my head and headed for the stairway; the blast through the door was like a furnace.

On July 18, 1945, the estate of Ruth Lyon Andrews settled for $6,000; the estate of Mrs. Price eventually settled, reportedly at $10,000 or $12,000.

By April 14, repair work on 110 rooms had started and was expected to be completed within two months. The cost was estimated at $65,000. Six months later, on October 25, 1944, the fireproofing of The Jefferson was completed.

The fire also produced a flurry of petty crime. Like a mob looting under the cover of a riot, a man named Blair Cox, thirty-three, stole personal items immediately after the fire from at least a dozen rooms on the fifth and sixth floors. Guests with items missing included Dr. H.B. Stewart, of Baltimore, who reported a watch and $271 stolen, and hotel resident Paul Christian, who lived in Room 690, was out a watch and $41. R.S. Koonce was missing an Elgin wristwatch valued at $40 and a quart of scotch, and Captain Henry L. Downing Jr. of the Richmond Army Air Base had an automatic pistol and gasoline coupons stolen.

The day after the fire—Saturday, March 11—was the last day the Virginia House of Delegates met for the year. The pastor from Ginter Park Baptist Church offered the opening prayer. Joint House and Senate Resolutions were approved expressing condolences for the family of Aubrey Gardner Weaver. "The State of Virginia," the resolution proclaimed, "has sustained a loss…impossible to measure in the death of this outstanding citizen and leader." A House Joint Resolution proclaimed that Mrs. Lillian Martin Price "caused all who knew her to admire and respect her for her many fine qualities." House members approved leave of absence from the March 11 session for Messrs. DeJarnette and Davis, their colleagues injured in the fire.

In May 1946, the Federated Welfare Humane Society held its semiannual luncheon meeting with the theme of humane education. The group awarded a medal to Sandy, a dog owned by eleven-year-old Russell Bowles. Sandy had spent more than a year assisting marines during World War II. Approximately 892 dogs (of which at least 57 were named

Duke) "volunteered" and served as "devildogs" with the marines during World War II. Upon enlisting, they were shipped to the Dog Detachment Training Center at Camp Lejeune, North Carolina, where—like regular marines—they received training, personnel files and ranks.

The topic of soldiers and The Jefferson came up again in a *Times Dispatch* story in February 1946. In as unique a note of appreciation as you may ever hear, Lieutenant Joseph Greene expressed thanks to The Jefferson—a hotel he had probably never been to or even heard of before—and promised to stay there if he ever got to Richmond. During the war, when he was deep in the jungle, two hundred miles from the nearest village, Lieutenant Greene found a Jefferson Hotel towel. Finding a Jefferson towel is always a good thing, but this find was especially fortuitous because at that time he was wounded and greatly in need of something to use as a bandage.

Winston Churchill visited Richmond in March 1946, smoking his cigar and flashing his famous "V" salute as he rode in an open car. With General Eisenhower next to him, Churchill addressed the Virginia House of Delegates. He loved Richmond and called Monument Avenue "one of the most beautiful avenues of the world." Sixty years later, in 2006, Churchill was named an honorary Virginian.

To get an idea how much a room cost in the postwar years, a guest in December 1946 paid $5.50 for a room. Another guest spent $2.25 a night in June 1947.

V

New Owners

On October 24, 1947, Colonel Charles Consolvo, owner of all Jefferson corporation stock, died. His obituary ran in papers all over America, including the *New York Times*, which had frequently reported about him over the years. The last photograph of "America's number one circus fan" shows him resting his right arm on a clown's shoulder, with the forlorn stare of an old circus man who knows the big top is packing up to leave town.

Governor Tuck of Virginia was one of the estimated thousand mourners at the funeral. Jefferson Hotel manager A. Gerald Bush was a pallbearer. Sidney Banks, a future hotel co-owner, was an honorary pallbearer. At 10:30 a.m. on the day of the funeral—October 27, 1947—all Virginia hotels were supposed to dim their lights for five minutes in tribute to the colonel. Bernard November, a retired Baltimore businessman, stepped in to run Consolvo's businesses until their disposition.

Most of Consolvo's estate—estimated at $2 million—was divided between two Norfolk charities: St. Mary's Female Orphanage (also known as the Infant Home) and DePaul Hospital. The estate had three main holdings to sell: the outdoor advertising agency, which quickly went for $425,000 to John Donnelly and Sons, which planned to replace the company's 1,800 wooden billboards with modern all-metal types; Norfolk's Monticello Hotel, with an asking price of $2 million; and finally, The Jefferson Hotel.

Consolvo and a clown. Consolvo had run off to the circus as a kid. *Courtesy of Sargeant Memorial Collection, Norfolk Public Library.*

Taxes paid upon the transfer of Consolvo's estate in 1948 revealed that The Jefferson was valued at $698,410 ($543,410 for land and building and $155,000 for furnishings and fixtures). The hotel was making money. *Commonwealth Magazine* reported 1949 net sales of $369,366. Consolvo's executors sold the hotel for $650,000 on April 25, 1949, to the Cavalier Hotel Corporation, which consisted of Sidney Banks, president; Fred E. Watkins, vice-president; Albert Suttle Sr., vice-president; and George Suttle, secretary/treasurer.

The new owners were short of cash to close at settlement. So they did what anyone who desperately needed cash (this being before ATMs) who owned a hotel would do: they borrowed it from the hotel's cash drawers. Problem solved. They were able to close, but that created a new problem. For several hours until the bank opened the next day, the hotel was completely out of cash. To get an idea of what a dollar was worth at that time, Thanksgiving dinner at the hotel in 1949, including a bowl of clear green turtle soup, cost $2.50. By September 14, 1949, the Cavalier Hotel Corporation had legally merged names with the Hotel Jefferson Corporation to become the Cavalier-Jefferson Corporation.

Owners and manager, circa 1953. *From left*: Sidney Banks, Fred Watkins, Al Suttle Sr. and James Powell. *Courtesy of Sue Powell Williams.*

THANKSGIVING

DINNER $2.50

CHOICE

Oysters on Half Shell   Chilled Juices
Fruit Cocktail   Shrimp Cocktail
Caviar Canape   Iced Casaba Melon

Cream of Chicken Noodle Soup   Clear Green Turtle Soup

Toasted Almonds, Celery, Olives and Relish Tray

ENTREE

Filet of Bass, Shrimp, Mushrooms and Oysters, Marguery
Roast Stuffed Virginia Turkey, Giblet Gravy
Baked Smithfield Ham, Champagne Sauce
Roast Choice Ribs of Beef, au jus

CHOICE

Broccoli   New Peas   Onions in Cream
Candied Sweet Yams   Mashed Potatoes

SALAD

Princess Salad, Mayonnaise

CHOICE

Pumpkin Pie   Mince Meat Pie   Apple Pie
Plum Pudding Brandy Sauce   Cheese and Crackers
Ice Cream   Sherbet

Mints

Coffee   Tea   Milk

SPECIAL $1.25

Hot Turkey Sandwich, Cranberry Sauce
Mashed Potatoes   New Peas
Bread, Butter, Choice of Drinks

Thanksgiving menu, 1949.
Courtesy of Mary Stuart Cruickshank.

A *Richmond Times Dispatch* story in April 1949 also listed Gerould McLean Rumble and Harry Rumble III as officers. Gerould M. Rumble, the Norfolk attorney in charge of closing the loan, had serious ethical problems, to put it gently. He embezzled $19,875.40 from the new owners. On October 1, 1952, the hotel sued the Connecticut Mutual Life Insurance Company to recover the money. The insurance company, the entity responsible for paying 1949 real estate taxes, had given the money to Rumble to pay, but Rumble kept it. The day after the suit was filed, the fifty-five-year-old lawyer killed himself. On February 5, 1954, The Jefferson-Cavalier Corporation learned it had lost the suit.

One thing of note that occurred between the time Consolvo died and the new owners took over was that on April 15, 1948, it was reported the last Jefferson alligator died of old age. Hotel manager A. Gerald Bush said he wasn't sure if the alligator would be replaced.

Albert Suttle Sr.

Born in January 1907, Albert Suttle (no middle name), along with his eight brothers and two sisters, was raised in Newport News, Virginia, where his father ended up after arriving in America from Lebanon at the turn of the century. His father, Michael Suttle, opened a bicycle shop in Newport News in 1901, eventually adding on to also make it a gunsmith shop and an automobile service station. He was one of the few people skilled at the difficult work of putting vulcanized rubber onto automobile wheels. He lost a hand in an automobile accident, forcing Albert and his older brother George to stop their education and go to work in the business.

In 1931, Chevrolet revoked the franchise of the man who managed its Petersburg dealership, offering Albert the opportunity to manage it. Albert knew everything about cars and mechanics. He could take cars apart and put them back together. So at the start of the Depression, young Albert packed up and moved to Petersburg to run Master Chevrolet Sales. It was at the dealership where he met his future wife, an employee he had hired. In 1941, the dealership started selling Cadillacs, but the sign out front always said Chevrolet. They usually had about fifty employees and at one point as many as sixty-five. In 1972, they started sponsoring NASCAR driver Lennie Pond, who ended up winning NASCAR Rookie of the Year. The sponsorship—which consisted of providing a one-ton truck and up to $10,000 in auto parts—continued for 1973 and 1974.

Albert Suttle Sr., hotel co-owner, 1949–83. *Courtesy of Ray Hash Photography.*

Two things become very clear when looking at Albert Suttle. First, his personality traits: he was very honest and modest. Someone told me he was almost too good to be in business, "almost too straight-laced." After World War II ended, Suttle, unlike many auto dealers at the time, wouldn't take a little cash on the side to move customers up the list to buy a new automobile. The war had temporarily put a halt to automobile production, so there was a keen demand for new automobiles after the war, with many dealerships having waiting lists.

The other trait was ambition. Suttle was a workaholic, a stickler for details and an incredibly busy man. He did not know down time. He was involved in all kinds of business ventures, mostly with his partner, Fred Watkins. It's not known how they came together to form a partnership, but Albert Jr. speculated that his father might have empathized with Watkins because, like his father, Watkins had also lost a hand in an accident. Watkins lost his hand in a farming accident. They occasionally socialized at Virginia Beach, where they each had beach cabanas at the Cavalier Beach Club. The Beach Club was part of the Cavalier Hotel, a hotel they co-owned. They had extensive real estate holdings, including the Keswick Country Club, outside Charlottesville, and the Cavalier-Lauderdale in Fort Lauderdale, Florida. In March 1946, Suttle, Fred Watkins and Alvin Hechler (a Chevy dealer in Highland Springs) were named by a court to manage a new company—Consolidated Dairy Farms Inc.—formed to handle the extensive financial holdings of Hugh Rakes. Rakes, once credited with being the largest individual dairy producer in the United States, went into bankruptcy, with his remaining proceeds going to creditors. Suttle was also a longtime board member of a Petersburg bank and, in 1957, was appointed chairman of the Richmond-Petersburg Turnpike Authority. He was exceptionally active in business, as well as many fraternal and religious organizations such as the Elks, his church and the Commonwealth Club.

All through The Jefferson years, Suttle ran his Chevrolet dealership full time and made only occasional trips to The Jefferson to check on operations. He took his family to dinner there every couple months, a dress-up affair in the mezzanine dining area. Suttle died in 1995, the year of the hotel's centennial anniversary.

FRED E. WATKINS

Fred Ernest Watkins, born in 1903, got into the car business in 1927, eventually selling Cadillacs, Oldsmobiles and Chevrolets at his dealership in South Hill, Virginia. One person characterized Watkins, a man with an innate ability to spot business opportunities, as kind and direct but gruff if you didn't know him. At one time, Watkins may have owned more land in the state of Virginia than any other individual. Watkins had lost an arm in a sawmill accident. Watkins had said that losing his arm was a blessing—it forced him to use his mind rather than his hands.

His daughter, Betsy Watkins Short, described him as a soft-spoken, large man, six feet, three or four inches, with a fifth-grade education. His word meant everything, and he believed written contracts were unnecessary. Somewhere along the line, probably through selling cars, he met and went into business with Albert Suttle. Mrs. Short doesn't know how her father met Sidney Banks, the "hotel man of the group," with Watkins and Suttle being the money guys. The connection might have been that they both owned houses in Virginia Beach—Banks lived there, and Watkins had a summer home there. Watkins kept a room at The Jefferson for his visits to Richmond; Mrs. Short thinks it was Room 630. An employee who worked at the hotel in 1980 told me that the sixth floor was closed off at that time to the general public. Watkins had frequent business in Richmond, but the trips to The Jefferson were more or less just to check in. He died in October 1986.

Watkins was a member of the Rotunda Club, and his wife was a member of the Colony Club. Mrs. Short had her wedding rehearsal dinner in the Colony Club in June 1958 and her wedding reception at The Jefferson. She knew the Federal Reserve tried to buy the hotel and planned to tear it down, but her father adamantly opposed selling it. He had a love for history and old buildings, and he did not want the building torn down. She said it had gotten to the point where Watkins and Suttle wanted out but wanted to sell to someone who would keep the building. Watkins was more involved with the hotel business than Suttle but less than Sidney Banks.

Sidney Banks

Sidney Banks was born in Bland County, Virginia, in 1898 and died in Fort Lauderdale in 1989. He was five feet, seven inches tall and intensely charismatic. Like Suttle and Watkins, he was also a very busy man, but unlike Suttle and Watkins, he focused almost all his efforts on the hotel business. Sidney Banks was the consummate hotel man. In a sense, he grew up in the business, watching his father, who owned hotels in Virginia and West Virginia.

At the very young age (young for hotel years) of thirty-one, Banks became the manager of the Princess Anne Country Club in 1927. In 1931, when Suttle was starting his car dealership, Banks was appointed managing director of the Cavalier Hotel in Virginia Beach. He had owned and managed several hotels, including the Chamberlain, before teaming up with Suttle and Watkins to buy The Jefferson in 1949. Banks's original connection to the hotel business might have run right through the circus. Like Charles Consolvo, perhaps the preeminent Virginia hotel man in the first half of the twentieth century, Banks had also been involved with the circus, doing accounting work.

His son Walter told me that Sidney Banks had pretty much given up his hobby of golf to work exclusively on hotel business. He loved working with hotel guests and employees. Banks didn't go to college but did acquire a wide array of unique experiences through many odd jobs. He ran power lines through North Carolina, a very difficult and challenging task when you think about doing such a thing from scratch, not simply replacing existing power lines.

Banks actively ran the Cavalier Hotel until March 1960, when he sold it and other property for $2.2 million. It appears Banks had a falling out with Watkins and Suttle. A newspaper story identified Banks's three "new" associates, making Suttle and Watkins his former associates. Banks wanted out, and Watkins and Suttle were OK with him leaving.

After buying The Jefferson with Watkins and Suttle in 1949, Banks and his family moved into the hotel for about eight months to keep close tabs on the renovations. His son Walter enjoyed riding his bicycle in the halls and especially loved the room service. He didn't recall any alligators, proving with 100 percent certainty that the alligators were gone by then. A kid living at the hotel would have known about them and would remember them years later. Sidney Banks later bought the Lago Mar Hotel in Fort Lauderdale, which is now owned by his son Walter and his grandchildren.

It's not known which of the three—Suttle, Watkins or Banks—stopped in 1954 to pick up a nineteen-year-old hitchhiker named Don James. At the time, Don James was a U.S. Navy corpsman stationed at the naval hospital in Portsmouth, Virginia. One weekend, he tried to hitchhike back home to Buffalo, New York, but didn't make it because of a paralyzing snowstorm. He had to turn around and head back to Portsmouth to get back to work on a Monday but found himself out of money and very hungry. The kid got picked up by a gentleman in a luxury car, likely a Cadillac. During the course of the conversation, he learned that the driver was an owner of The Jefferson Hotel. James wasn't very impressed because he was a nineteen-year-old kid who had never heard of the hotel. It was late Saturday night. The driver—Suttle, Watkins or Banks—gave James money to take a bus back, but he was so hungry he ended up using it for food. James recalled that hitchhiking back at that point was easy because he finally had food in his stomach. In 2011, Don James wrote to the hotel to share this story, claiming, "I never, in all these years, forgot this man's generosity. At the time, to me, he was a life saver."

MANAGEMENT OPERATIONS

The new owners immediately started a $600,000 restoration project. Shortly after that was announced, they began a $150,000 "face-lifting," with the work done by Philadelphia interior decorator Henry H. Holmead. The newsstand in the Rotunda (referred to as the main lobby) adjacent to the Main Street entrance would become part of a soda fountain. Both alligator pools next to The Jefferson Statue would be filled in to make a new special function room. A renovation was surely needed. The *Richmond News Leader* ran an April 1949 editorial suggesting that The Jefferson

> *should be refurbished and supplied with long-needed new plumbing fixtures. Its bedrooms, in short, should be put on par with its lobbies and its Franklin Street parlors…From the opening of the hotel, its food was superlative until almost the First World War. Many Richmonders can recall a time when the main dining room on the Main Street front was crowded nightly, and scarcely a vacant table could be found in the beautiful palm garden restaurant…We believe that many persons…will patronize a restored and glorified Jefferson café.*

A. Gerald Bush, who had stayed on as manager after the hotel was sold in 1949, retired on October 19, 1951. William H. (Bill) Caldwell, who got started in the hotel business as a dishwasher in his hometown of Ripley, Tennessee, replaced Bush as manager. Caldwell's tenure was amazingly brief. On January 24, 1952, less than three months later, James Malvern

Powell, forty-one, was named general manager to replace Caldwell. The announcement was made by Banks. Powell got his start in the hotel business in public relations at the Chamberlin at Old Point Comfort, on the grounds of Fortress Monroe in Hampton, Virginia.

A reporter named William Bien of the *Richmond News Leader* wrote a delightfully entertaining biographical piece about James "Jimmie" Powell, "typical of today's professional hotel executive—polished to a smooth, rich gloss; trained to make 'no' sound like 'yes'; able to make the most extraordinary requests seem trivial; and endowed with the patience of Job." Powell started every day with a morning walk through the entire hotel, "a building with mysterious towers to delight a child's fancy and history fairly screaming from every shadowed corner." Past each of the four hundred rooms, up one hallway and down the next, from the sixth floor to the basement, Powell spent his first half hour this way before getting to his duties: "There are dozens of letters to be answered personally each morning…meetings with some or all of the hotel's 215 employees…conferences with any of 15 department heads…hands to be shaken—$1,000-a-day payrolls to be checked…101 details every day." Powell credited his wife, Helen Gwaltney Norfleet Powell, otherwise known

James Powell, hotel manager, 1952–61. *Courtesy of Sue Powell Williams.*

simply as Bunny: "I was lucky. A hotel manager is out of luck if his wife isn't understanding, or doesn't have the knack of getting along with people. She can be a tremendous asset." Most people would envy Powell's "duty" of greeting famous guests such as Henry Fonda or Humphrey Bogart, but what none of them know "is often there are harried moments when he'd gladly change places with anyone—but, being the good hotel man, he'll never let it show."

Powell's daughter, Sue Powell Williams, has very fond memories of living at the hotel as a kid. I met her on a chilly morning at a hotel where her son, Jay Williams, is the assistant general manager. There's something satisfying to know that a longtime hotel man like James Powell has a grandson in hotel management. You know the guy, who spent his entire career in the field and seemed to thoroughly enjoy it, would be proud. Sue showed up with two big scrapbooks—a bonanza of rich details—snugly placed in plastic to protect against the drizzling rain. Fortunately for history, people like Sue Powell Williams spent hours putting scrapbooks together and then decades preserving them. In 1952, she moved into The Jefferson Hotel, Room 312—with her mother, father, brother and dog— in four rooms strung together to form a large suite. She loved everything about it from the time she moved in to the day she moved out several years later, after she got married. Roller-skating in the ballroom, sorting mail behind the registration desk, ordering room service whenever her parents were away at a party or event—what's not to love for a kid? She even operated the telephone switchboard, magically plugging all those wires into their respective places on the enormous board, a challenging job for anyone, especially a teenager. She had been around hotels so long that she could do things like that. Sometime she and her brother, Jim, got driven to school by a driver in her dad's pink Cadillac, and if that weren't enough, the chauffeur occasionally took Sue and her friends to movies and then back to The Jefferson for a sleepover. This was very cool, or whatever the term used back in the 1950s was. Grade school was at Ginter Park, named for the man who built The Jefferson. She loved the family dinners, every night at 6:00 p.m. sharp on the mezzanine, same table—the one in the southeast corner. No matter how busy her father was, he always joined them for dinner. Breakfast in the Colonial Coffee Shop, in a room to the east side of the Rotunda— almost always coke and a chicken sandwich, an unusual breakfast choice perhaps, but so what? She was a teenager. The coffee shop was near the writing room, in the northeast corner of the Rotunda. The writing room contained one desk in the middle with four chairs; the walls were papered with a colonial scene, something you might see in Williamsburg today.

She loved everything about living at the hotel. "It was a wonderful time," she says more than once, and you can see her eyes light up when she thinks about it. On Christmas night each year, the Powells packed up and went to the Cavalier-Lauderdale in Florida to spend the holidays. Sue Powell fondly recalls the years she was selected as the Miller & Rhoads "Snow Queen." The M&R Santa, Bill Strother, stayed at The

Jefferson during the Christmas seasons. She said her mother was almost as important to managing the hotel as her father. They worked together as a team. Her family was very close to Sidney Banks's family; she called Sidney Banks "Uncle Sidney."

The business of running the hotel continued, albeit with more of a focus toward the clubs and to permanent residents rather than overnight guests. This period was like the last half of a long airplane flight after the food has been served, the plastic plates discarded, the lights turned off—sort of on autopilot waiting to start the descent.

On March 22, 1950, a dance and fashion show at The Jefferson, with prizes for the best-dressed man and woman of the University of Richmond, was "pre-televised" by Station WMBG. Harvey Hudson and Patsy Garrett, formerly with Fred Waring's Orchestra, sang and did commentary. Climax Beverage Company distributed ginger ale, and Philip Morris handed out cigarettes. In April 1950, the Historic Garden Week of Virginia put on its annual garden show, as usual, with its headquarters in Room 1 of The Jefferson. On January 22, 1950, you could dance to the music of Don McGrane and His Orchestra in the Empire Room; every Wednesday that month was "Arthur Murray Night." In December, holiday revelers enjoyed The Jefferson Jubilee Singers perform Christmas carols. If all that wasn't enough music, you could hear the Four Brothers or Paul Sparr and His Orchestra.

This would have been about the same time that Bernie Wayne composed "Blue Velvet." He had been staying at The Jefferson in 1951 while visiting friends in Richmond and penned the lyrics after seeing a beautiful woman at a hotel party. The song became a huge hit for Tony Bennett and later Bobby Vinton. The Women's Division of Hotel Greeters exchanged pleasantries at its June 1952 convention. With more than four thousand members, the group had been around since about 1921. Miss Virginia Pearson was reelected president.

Guest folios from February 1951 reveal that a room cost $7.00. In August 1951, one guest paid $10.00 for a room at The Jefferson—"The showplace of the South." An advertisement from September 1952 shows room rates "from $4.00 with bath." An October 1952 advertisement reveals that dinners at The Jefferson cost $1.50. For $0.90, kids had their choice of three TV dinners (called TV Delights): the Hopalong Cassidy, the Little Miss Muffet or the Howdy Doody.

The Virginia for Eisenhower Committee set up headquarters at The Jefferson in January 1952; its first task was to get more of the "I Like

Postcard, Main Street, 1950s. *Courtesy of The Jefferson Hotel.*

Ike" buttons that were in such high demand. The committee welcomed contributions "from a dollar up." The Virginia Aberdeen-Angus Association had its annual bull session, with the address given by Admiral Lewis Strauss, chairman of the Atomic Energy Commission and owner of Brandy Rock Farm in Culpeper County. The *Richmond Times Dispatch* reported that Strauss had not told the group whether he would talk about atoms or Angus cattle: "He's considered an authority on each subject." In September 1953, Eleanor Roosevelt sent a thank-you note to Manager Powell for making her stay during the United Nations conference a pleasant one.

An ad from the early 1950s boasted that fifty rooms were cooled with Mitchell air-conditioning units, "the world's finest." In June 1953, The Jefferson was completing the three-year, $600,000 improvement program, which included redecorating and new plumbing. Most exciting of all, however, was that one hundred rooms would be outfitted with the very modern electronic device called a television. New elevators were installed, and a sun porch was put in on the west roof at the sixth floor. In addition, a 278-foot carpet—costing more than $10,000—was installed on the mezzanine. To complete the renovation, a new gift and antique shop, as well as a new coffee shop, was opened. The *Richmond News Leader* reported that Manager Powell recalled with a sigh:

> *Guests and casual visitors, many of whom feel that they have a proprietary interest in the establishment, still insist on moving a vase of flowers from one table to another and demand that draperies be adjusted to suit their notions of how the lobby ought to look. And he has a fat file of letters—comments, suggestions, praise and criticism—from hundreds of persons discussing such departures from tradition as the abolition of the alligator pools and the installation of a television set at the base of The Jefferson Statue in the Palm Court. (The management stood firm on its decision that the alligators must go, but it yielded to public pressure for Jefferson's statue to be protected against competition for public interest by the TV set.)*

In April 1958, with plans to put in another $100,000 in improvements, Manager Powell said the hotel had had its best year ever and had grossed over $1 million in revenue every year since 1952. In 1952 and 1953, gross profits stood at $1.06 million and $1.03, respectively. Here are some figures for those years:

	1952	**1953**
Gross Profit	$1,064,473.66	$1,032,962.93
Net Profit	$87,879.06	$24,733.63
Average Spent Daily, Per Guest	$4.42	$4.57
Percentage of Occupancy	74.09	72.56
Total Payroll	$245,816.80	$243,680.05
Real Estate Taxes	$17,648.72	$17,768.55
Coal	$12,230.64	$10,778.83
Electricity	$18,619.86	$19,557.29
Insurance	$5,378.24	$5,360.51
Postage	$942.87	$834.49
Legal Expenses	$1,953.20	$1,710.97
Telephone and Telegrams	$718.39	$1,095.90
Advertising and Business Promotions	$30,029.46	$32,650.01
Mortgage Interest	$26,952.73	$25,371.01

Each year, the hotel spent about $8,640 on water and $2,930 on oil. The printing department used 180 pounds of ink annually to print, among other things, 23,480 dinner menus and 69,680 luncheon menus.

Since this isn't a financial or accounting text, I'll spare you many more details, but here are the wages paid for the month of December 1953 to various kitchen employees: the two bakers (combined) got $517.55 that month; the four cooks, $1,008.33; one oyster-opener, $189; and the ten waiters and waitresses received a total of $646.99.

Much of the hotel's income was derived by renting space to various organizations. The following represents income earned from some of the concessions and rentals for 1953:

Florist	$1,800.00
Virginia Highways Users	$1,830.48
Cigar Stand and Soda Bar	$6,794.34
L.B. Price	$300.00
Beauty Shop	$1,200.00
Gift Shop	$3,677.41
Associate Discount Corporation	$5,100.00
Gemmill Insurance Agency	$1,200.00
Rotunda Club	$20,000.04
Press Club	$416.67
Wright Brokerage	$915.00
Cabell Eanes, Inc.	$3,000.00
Thalhimer's	$1,529.65
Clair Nichols	$225.00
Traveler's Protective Association	$913.56
Crozet & Co.	$350.00
Barber Shop	$414.86
Marco Hearing Aid	$420.00
World Book	$593.75

The small amount paid by the Press Club was due to the fact that the club had just moved in. Three years later, it paid $1,550 for the year. From 1952 to 1953, the hotel lost the rental income from the Eisenhower Headquarters ($600), an organization called Battery Life ($1,825) and Phillips-Manzer & Stringfellow ($2,400).

The owners of The Jefferson Hotel were actively acquiring new businesses in the mid-1950s. In July 1955, they bought the Country Club of Keswick at Charlottesville and a few months later acquired a hotel in Fort Lauderdale, Florida, which they remodeled and renamed the Lauderdale-Cavalier.

THE KID FIXES THE CLOCKS

Things might have been going well financially for the hotel, but apparently not well enough to spend the money needed to get the two clocks in the towers working again. Rising 172 feet above Main Street, the faces of the clocks are more than six feet in diameter, with the pendulum more than thirteen feet. They had been broken for more than a decade. The Jefferson Hotel wasn't going to pay to get them fixed, so maybe the kid could take a look. Some of the women who lived at the hotel took it upon themselves to locate the twelve-year-old boy with a skill for fixing old clocks. At the time, Allen Barringer, who lived on Hanover Street, had recently been written about in a newspaper story for getting the clock at Pace Memorial Methodist Church working again.

In the summer of 1954, Allen Barringer might have been the most popular kid in Richmond or, for that matter, the state of Virginia. What other twelve-year-old kid was allowed to do something as adventurous as ride his bike over to the grand old Jefferson and climb up immense clock towers? Normally, this type of fun and excitement—after all, that's exactly how a kid would see it—is something kids would do only to be chased away by adults with threats that the police would be called next time. But twelve-year-old Allen Barringer was not only allowed to make these fun trips up the towers, but he was also *asked* to do so by hotel management. In August 1954, Allen Barringer rode fast and furiously from his home (in what's now fashionably called the Fan District), often with his buddy Sean Kilpatrick, climbing up the twin clock towers to clear them of pigeon nests and debris.

It was not easy to get up those towers, either. Barringer said it was not something you wanted to do alone. "They were dark and dusty… climbing through the dark levels below you might spook any number of pigeons and…the other living things lurking." It's pretty remote up there. A newspaper story from 1956 reported that a six-foot tree was growing in the concrete of one of the clock towers. To get up to the clocks, you have to climb iron ladders fastened to the brick, and the first step is set quite high. It's not made for the average person to climb, certainly not a kid. The ladder steps are not on an angle, like the folded ladders you might think of when you think of ladders. These steps are perfectly vertical, so you have to pull your weight straight up. I went up there and understand why the hotel doesn't want anyone up there. It's like you're in an obstacle course, but without soft

Clock tower. *Courtesy of James Oliver Images.*

grass or dirt below you. Everything around you is brick, asphalt and steel—unforgiving, hard objects.

Today, Allen Barringer is a retired attorney with fond memories of his bicycle trips with his buddies to the clock towers. He modestly claimed that anyone who could fix a bicycle could have fixed those clocks—they just needed the pigeon nests and debris cleared out and the clocks oiled. Once they got the clocks working again, all that was needed was to wind them once a week. He recalled that the hotel people had a lot of difficulty figuring out how to get up to the towers, and for a long time they couldn't find the key to open the door leading to the roof. Eventually, they found the key but realized they didn't need it at all. He recalls the hotel as pretty seedy at the time, but it was still a grand old hotel. The eastern tower housed the master clock that controlled the other tower clock, as well as all twenty-four clocks throughout the hotel. The western clock needed a replacement battery as the power source to obtain the signal from the eastern clock. Barringer's father (who worked for the telephone company) wrestled up an old discarded twenty-four-volt battery from the telephone company. After closing the tower windows on each trip, Barringer found them mysteriously reopened on subsequent trips. It turns out that Jefferson employees had been going up there for squab—a delicacy worthy of the finest restaurants.

The clock boy shared with me the nickname his friends tagged him with in 1954: "Tic-Toc." He was honored by the National Association of Watch and Clockmakers with a one-year membership and almost got to meet President Eisenhower. At the last minute, Ike passed on the photo-op, forcing Barringer and his father to settle for a private White House tour. Barringer recalls begging his father to leave the tour as quickly as possible so they could go to a nearby Washington, D.C. magic shop.

Hotel Manager Powell gave Barringer a twenty-five-dollar savings bond. Several international newspapers, including the *Sydney* [Australia] *Morning Herald* picked up the story about the boy fixing the clocks. For years afterward, he received the watchmakers' newsletters, which discussed all things related to clocks and allowed him to order hard-to-find parts needed to make repairs. Later, he made a few dollars by fixing broken clocks for neighbors and people who had heard about him. The calls continued for several years, including one request that came in after Barringer had gone away to college. Getting paid to fix clocks, Barringer reported, "beat mowing lawns and newspaper delivery by a mile."

Gibson Worsham masterfully summarized the role of the clocks in an essay about The Jefferson's architecture: "The provision of public clocks as a civic amenity had long been a function of major public buildings such as courthouses and churches. Here, by their ubiquity and opulence, they proclaimed a regulatory role for the hotel in Richmond's social life."

In the early photographs and drawings of the hotel, you can see American flags flying from each of the clock towers. It's not known how long the flags flew, but the flagpoles came down on May 12, 1971, when Johnny Cowan marched up a 220-foot crane to remove the poles on both towers. The pole on the western tower had been leaning precariously.

ELVIS IN RICHMOND

You could write a book about Elvis in Richmond and put out a thick volume even if you just stuck to the first six months of 1956. In that short period, Elvis made three trips to Richmond, performing each time at the Mosque. By that time, most Americans knew about him, but there were still many who didn't, including a couple hotel patrons who didn't seem to notice him on June 30 as he walked through The Jefferson Hotel carrying an RCA "Transistor Seven" radio, which looked "like a briefcase with knobs on it." The youth of Richmond had previously seen the future rock-and-roll king on February 5 and March 22 of that year. But in late June, Bill Railey, owner of Railey's Appliance Record and Store, brought the young musician, along with his stage show, to perform. For $2.50, you could have relaxed beforehand knowing you had a seat reserved for you when you got there. General admission patrons paid $1.50.

Alfred Wertheimer, a New York photographer following Elvis as he toured, wrote about the shows in Richmond. Those performances are still discussed by Elvis fans today because they generated a couple very captivating photos. When later asked why he chose to spend so much time covering this budding celebrity, Wertheimer said it was because Elvis "permitted closeness and made the girls cry." The screaming girls "had crossed over into the region of the possessed and the saved."

To have a place to hang out that Saturday before the concerts, Elvis and his cousin "Junior" rested up at The Jefferson Hotel, described by Wertheimer as "a Southern mixture of ancient Greece, Florentine Italy and King Arthur's Court." Elvis, wearing a dignified slate-gray suit, pressed white shirt and white knit tie, stopped with Junior at the hotel coffee shop. The radio "rested silently next to a bowl of chili." To anyone looking in at the time, there was nothing unique about the coffee shop or about Elvis. Black-and-white photos, however, didn't capture the vivid color. The shop had a row of red vinyl chairs, and a pair of white bucks adorned Elvis's feet. A breakfast of bacon, eggs over-easy, milk, no coffee and home fries, capped off with a scoop of vanilla ice cream in cantaloupe, infused Elvis with the fuel needed for the shows.

Years later, waitress Alice Davis recalled serving Elvis twice in her thirty-seven years of service, once when he was coming up and the next time "when he was big." She said Elvis was "a very, very shy young man" and "one of the nicest people you'd ever want to meet." The hotel manager was appalled that Elvis picked up bacon with his fingers. Sue Powell Williams, the manager's daughter, recalls seeing Elvis check into the hotel carrying his own television set.

A lot of people—famous, infamous and just plain common—passed through The Jefferson. Of course, conventions kept coming, too. In April 1956, the Philip Morris Company sponsored a contest to award a three-speed phonograph at The Jefferson to the University of Richmond fraternity collecting the most cigarettes wrappers during a five-week period. In November 1956, the Chesapeake Bay Yacht and Racing Association held its annual meeting at The Jefferson. At about this time, the fifty members of the local chapter of Greek Orthodox Youth of America met. Activities included a basketball game, an icebreaker dance and a movie.

In 1957, the Virginia State Nurses Association met, as did the Virginia State Printers Association, whose sixth annual meeting included something called "a shirt-sleeve conference." Perhaps this meant they didn't have to wear jackets or ties, the 1950s version of what later became casual Fridays. At the banquet, Miss Rebecca Richardson of Martinsville was crowned "Miss Perfect Type."

The Richmond Advertising Club had its first seminar at the hotel. One of its meetings included a "brainstorming" session (with the quotations in the story). An originator of this new technique was going to explain it. In March 1957, the First Annual Convention of Defenders of State Sovereignty and Individual Liberties convened and issued a two-page "Declaration of Convictions," opposing "any

Rotunda from mezzanine. *Courtesy of Mary Stuart Cruickshank.*

Rotunda from ground level. *Courtesy of James Oliver Images.*

legislation designed to repose control of our educational system in the Federal Government" and "any effort to weaken further the immigration laws of America."

Some 5,000 members of the Loyal Order of the Moose attended a conference at the hotel, as did the Export-Import Club. The club heard Congressman J. Vaughn Gary tell it that Congress had cut $1.1 billion from President Eisenhower's original request of $3.9 billion for foreign aid, but that amount was still too much. About 200 delegates of the Sons of Confederate Veterans convened in November 1957, with James Jackson Kilpatrick of the *Richmond News Leader* speaking at the closing banquet. Also meeting in November was the Virginia Restaurant Association. Forty-five companies set up "elaborate and colorful displays of their products in the hotel ballroom." The association's president claimed that rising prices put the food industry in a tough squeeze. Food accounted for forty-eight cents out of each dollar, and labor took another thirty-two cents. The Reynolds Metals Company (RMC) rented a suite on the sixth floor in November 1957.

RMC was planning to transfer 350 employees and their families from Louisville, Kentucky, to Richmond. To assist the new arrivals, the five RMC employees in The Jefferson suite gathered all kinds of Richmond information—about schools, churches, shopping, real estate and even country clubs.

To benefit the Virginia Home for the Incurables Endowment Fund, the (eleventh annual) Tobacco Ball was held at The Jefferson on October 19, 1959; admission price: five dollars. This culminated in a weeklong festival to promote tobacco and raise money for youth. Tobacco balls were held every year from 1949 until 1983. E. Tucker Carlton, an architect, started the festival when he was an officer in Richmond's Optimist Club. At The Jefferson, local college students escorted the tobacco princesses—those selected in their towns or counties—who had traveled to Richmond, where one of them would be crowned Queen of Tobaccoland. The queen represented the tobacco industry for the next year at various conventions and meetings. Miss Judy Ann Austin of Sumter, South Carolina, reigned as the 1959 queen; she was described as weighing 116 pounds and standing five feet, five and a half inches tall. And in this 1950s reportage, an era of very long ago, her measurements were also provided for inquisitive readers: 36-24-36. In 1974, after twenty-three years, the festival had awarded $32,000 in college scholarships to the tobacco queens and $232,000 in charitable contributions. Frank Sinatra served as first grand marshal in 1949. Other grand marshals included actors James Arness and Eva Gabor; the comedians Rowan and Martin; writer Mickey Spillane; and baseball star Boog Powell. Tobacco balls were held—in late September or early October—at The Jefferson Hotel in 1953–57, 1959–62 and 1976. In other years, they were held at the John Marshall Hotel. Music in 1960 and 1961 was provided by the Meyer Davis Orchestra. An October 1951 story in the *New York Times* by James Kilpatrick mentioned that the festival, in its third year, "has become a fixture beyond the dreams of its sponsors."

On April 19, 1961, Marvin L. Moseley was named manager to replace James Powell, who left to manage the Sir Walter Hotel in Virginia Beach. Three years later, Moseley would make the papers by saying that The Jefferson wanted its annual Christmas party to be noncommercial, so there would be no Santa Claus.

VI

Private Clubs

The hotel was home at different times to four social clubs, where members were allowed to drink liquor so long as the liquor came from the members' own personal bottles kept in club lockers. Each club had an ABC Club license permitting this exception to the state liquor ban. The quality of the food served in the clubs, which all came from The Jefferson Hotel kitchen, was a constant source of irritation and displeasure, primarily because the service was consistently slow, and the clubs got whatever the hotel chose to put on the menu and paid whatever the hotel charged in the restaurant. Years later, one member recalled, "The large Jefferson Hotel kitchen…rarely provided the type of meals the club members desired." The clubs had to wait to be served. They had no special arrangement to get served first. A story in July 1955 boasted that kitchen service to the clubs had been added without increasing the number of hotel employees, a pretty good indication that service all around must have been pretty bad when you consider that The Jefferson kitchens—which were located in three different parts of the hotel—were serving the private clubs, the meals in the restaurants, room service and banquets and private parties.

Dan Booton, a Colony Club waiter, recalled that kitchen facilities were always a problem. The overworked chef labored sixteen hours a day. There were no elevators, so waiters had to carry trays through the back halls, and the halls were only wide enough to allow one waiter with a tray at a time. But it was so busy that the waiters needed to go back and forth at the same time, creating mishaps and many near-mishaps.

As of 1955, the clubs were paying an aggregate of $37,750 per year, of which $20,000 was coming from the Rotunda Club alone. Originally, the clubs leased about fourteen thousand square feet of hotel space. This figure jumped to about twenty-one thousand square feet when the Rotunda Club expanded in the late 1950s.

THE ROTUNDA CLUB[3]

The Rotunda Club came about as a direct result of the Commonwealth Club and the Country Club of Virginia announcing they had closed their waiting lists. A June 1949 *Richmond News Leaders* story reported:

> *It was understood that the move to found a new club resulted from "crowded" waiting lists at the Commonwealth Club and the Country Club of Virginia. It is known that the membership waiting lists at both of these clubs have been closed temporarily. A notice to members of the Country Club of Virginia informed them…all waiting lists for membership in the club have been closed temporarily. The notice was posted on May 25. A similar notice has been posted for the Commonwealth Club members. Men who have approached The Jefferson Hotel on the space situation have said it probably will take the Commonwealth Club seven or eight years to clear its long waiting list.*

Meetings to discuss a new private club to be located inside The Jefferson started in the fall of 1949. The original Rotunda Club officers were Franklin Trice, president; John G. Hayes Jr., vice-president; and Thomas C. Cauthorne, secretary/treasurer. The club opened in the spring of 1950 as a non-stock, nonprofit organization with 175 members. Before the Alcoholic Beverage Control (ABC) Board granted a license, however, it had to be assured that the club's rent would not be higher *because* of the ABC license, resulting in any pecuniary gain for the hotel owners. Club officials convinced ABC that its rent to The Jefferson Hotel would be no more than any other organization renting the same amount of space. With that assurance, ABC granted a license in June 1950.

---

3. Most of the information about the Rotunda Club comes from *The Rotunda Club* by Kathleen Fair and a *Richmond Times Dispatch* story by Joy Winstead.

The club took the space upstairs where the Palm Court and Lemaire Restaurant are located. In January 1958, Jefferson Hotel executive assistant manager Del Richardson replaced Gene Gilmartin as club manager. Thomas Herbert, the club's manager or "majordomo" for fifteen years, prided himself on remembering each member's food and drink preferences.

By the late 1950s—its heyday—the club boasted about five hundred members. A major five-year remodeling and expansion (from the original eight thousand square feet to fifteen thousand square feet), costing The Jefferson $100,000 and the club $20,000, was completed in the spring of 1958. The renovation opened up several small dining rooms, a parlor, a billiards room and a library. Unfortunately, however, the renovation closed off the Palm Court, resulting in a wall between the Palm Court and the top of the Grand Staircase. The Jefferson Statue was cut off from public view, meaning that people could see it only if they got someone in the club to let them in to see it.

Mrs. Juan Pletcher, manager for the club's last three years, said she escorted many hotel visitors to the private dining room to see the statue. Many have speculated that paint fumes from a Rotunda Club renovation killed the alligators, an impossible notion since the last alligator died in April 1948, more than a year before the discussion to form the club even started.

Generating the most controversy was the Men's Grill, a basement-level den where privacy ruled and the only women seen were the ones painted on canvas. An artist named Gari Melchers created several canvas masterpieces that hung on the walls from 1957 until 1961, when internal club dissension brought them down. Approximately 60 percent of club members voted in favor of keeping the paintings, but the more modest club members must have had the clout because their 40 percent minority votes counted more than those that voted to keep them. The paintings came down. One member called the Men's Grill "the den of manhood," and an overhead plaque read, "Independence Hall," as in independence from wives and girlfriends. There was even a secret exit onto Franklin Street where members could sneak out in those awkward moments when sneaking out was more preferable than staying in. Women, not the painted "Ladies of Independence Hall," but the real-life variety, gained official admittance once a year—at the Christmas party. In August 1989, twenty-eight years after the painted ladies had been removed from the club, The Jefferson exhibited four of them at the hotel.

By 1974, club membership stood at 306 active and 45 honorary members. Just three years later, it had dropped to a total of about

Grand Staircase, circa 1960. *Courtesy of Mary Stuart Cruickshank.*

230. The club tried to merge in 1976 with the much more established Commonwealth Club a couple blocks away. A commonality of note: Carrere & Hastings designed The Jefferson Hotel, as well as the Commonwealth Club. The Commonwealth Club urged its members to approve the merger: "The Board of Governors most earnestly

recommends your favorable vote." The July 22, 1976 letter stated that the Rotunda Club had at that time approximately 190 resident members and 42 nonresident members who were not with the Commonwealth Club. (Sixty members of the Rotunda Club held dual membership with the Commonwealth Club.) If the merger proposal passed, the Commonwealth would get the Rotunda Club members, as well as the $49,000 in the Rotunda Club's bank account. Three weeks later, the Commonwealth board announced that the proposed merger had been rejected and the plan was terminated. Eventually, on their own, 35 Rotunda Club members joined the Commonwealth Club.

The Rotunda Club voted in January 1977 to shut down. It worked aggressively with other clubs to get jobs at the same salary for its employees. To help the employees out financially, Rotunda Club members gave them money from the club's cash reserves—in amounts varying from hundreds to thousands of dollars. It's always tough getting laid off, especially so during a national economic disaster like the late 1970s. As a surprise treat, and to have a little fun, club members hosted a cocktail party in the last month. Turning the tables, the members acted as waiters, serving cocktails and hors d'ouevres to employees.

The Rotunda Club's grand finale farewell party, attended by more than two hundred members and guests, occurred on January 31, 1977. At three thirty in the morning, about forty hardcore partiers were still going when the band took the last request. It was "Proud Mary."

The next day, Valentine Auction Company sold the club's furnishings. After the auction, only a single folding table could be found. But when the final meal was served on that little table, it was covered with candelabra and finger bowls, and Harvey Louis wore white gloves to serve it. "The service was impeccable," Carl Sims, Rotunda Club manager, reported. "We went out in grand style."

THE COLONY CLUB[4]

The Colony Club—the women's club—opened on February 1, 1956. "With delicate colors and fresh flowers everywhere," one story

---

4. Most of the information about the Colony Club comes from a December 1968 *Richmond News Leader* story.

announced, "the Colony Club makes it easy to forget there are no windows, and that it occupies what was once The Jefferson's Turkish bath area." It was located in the northwest corner of the Rotunda level. Richmond residents paid thirty dollars for initiation and thirty-six dollars per year in dues; nonresidents paid fifteen dollars for initiation and twelve dollars per year in dues. Its four thousand square feet contained a main lounge and dining room decorated in eighteenth-century furnishings, a smaller lounge with early American furniture and another lounge in French provincial. The only contemporary—1950s, that is—decoration and furnishings were the card rooms, with bamboo chairs, tiled floors and bright draperies. The club's 1955 brochure included this description:

> *If you are one of the many women in Richmond who have desired a social club in which to relax with friends or to entertain at cards, dinner or cocktails—you will be delighted to know that a club offering such facilities to women is now organized: The Colony Club. And you are extended a cordial invitation to become a member. A spacious and attractive main lounge and dining room will be supplemented by six additional rooms of varying sizes. Also, there will be a cocktail lounge, powder rooms and a men's room. The entire club will be air-conditioned and sound-proofed. Luncheons, dinners and hors d'oeuvres will come from The Jefferson kitchens (as is done in the Rotunda Club for men). Food will be served at the regular prevailing prices.*

Mrs. Ernest H. Edinger and Mrs. William R. Trigg Jr. served as vice-presidents and Mrs. Wilfred A. Roper as president. In May 1964, the *Richmond News Leader* reported that eleven-year-old Marilyn Lee Roper pulled a cord to unveil a twenty-five- by thirty-inch portrait (done by Ann Pritchett) of her grandmother, Mrs. Roper, club president from 1955 to 1961.

The manager from the start was Dorothy J. Bender. Bender and her husband were co-chairs of the food, shelter and clothing unit of the disaster committee of the Chesterfield Chapter of the Red Cross. In addition, they were co-owners of the Half-Way House on the Petersburg Turnpike. All you need to know about the Half-Way House comes in this sentence from a December 1955 *Richmond News Leader* story: "The eating establishment located in the famous colonial tavern midway between Richmond and Petersburg, was one of three restaurants in this country to receive an award from the International

Epicurean Society, with headquarters in London." A later story about Mrs. Bender reported:

> *At the club she does just about everything—sets out flowers, does odd jobs, and clerical duties. She may be called to be a bartender, diplomat, florist, accountant, interior decorator, gourmet, etiquette expert and even a plumber. Promptly at 5 every day she goes up to her suite in the hotel and showers and changes for the dinner hour. She greets all the guests, and "whether it's a man or a woman, a guest must hear his name." Her husband picks her up at 8:30 p.m.*

Most club members were between sixty and seventy-five years old; the youngest was only twenty-seven, and the oldest was in her nineties. From 1957 through 1968, membership held steady at about 1,125. By 1974, membership had dropped to about 800, 8 of whom lived at The Jefferson. Members could bring friends and family to the club. The Christmas party and buffet in 1961 (price: five dollars) featured dancing to the music of Skeets Morris.

In 1978, after twenty-three years, the Colony Club closed out in high style, with a final Thanksgiving dinner bash. The *Richmond News Leader* reported, "Inflation, whiskey—by-the-drink and uncertainty about The Jefferson" led to the club's termination. At the end, the club had a month-to-month lease. The $150 initiation fee and $20 monthly dues in the late 1970s represented a fair amount of money at that time. The club's assets were auctioned off. The potential disruption of an upcoming planned renovation was cited as a reason the club had trouble getting new members. Manager Oakes was quoted as saying in November 1978 that he thought the hotel renovation would start within a year. Oakes said there were no plans to use the ten rooms formerly used by the Colony Club, but the idea of a nightclub appealed to him. The hotel was on the verge of shutting down, and he was thinking of opening a nightclub.

THE PRESS CLUB

The Press Club of Virginia—the first press club ever established in Virginia—was located on the first floor (Rotunda level) at Jefferson and Main Street, with two entrances. The brochure called the Press Club "an organization to promote the social and professional interests of men in the newspaper, radio-TV, public relations and allied fields."

The Jefferson Hotel paid $40,000 to convert the space to make up the Press Club. On December 5, 1953, more than one hundred club members first "inspected the lavish quarters...designed in a traditional Virginia style." They returned a week later for the club's first buffet supper. The club's 2,220 square feet boasted air-conditioning, a lounge, a bar room, a social room and a dining room with seating capacity for seventy-five. A mural by Fred Seibel, editorial cartoonist for the *Richmond Times Dispatch*, decorated one wall; another wall contained front-page mattes from leading Virginia newspapers. The club featured forums, luncheon speakers, bridge parties, summer fishing parties, Saturday night dances and an annual New Year's Eve dance.

James Powell, managing director of The Jefferson who "helped fan a flickering idea into a full flame," worked long and hard getting the club ready. James Baker of the *Richmond News Leader* credited Powell with getting things going: "He saw the need for a meeting place where news writers could sit down together in an atmosphere of congeniality and sociability to discuss their special interests, where they could gather to hear eminent men of their profession...and where they could go to get away from it all." Membership—by invitation only—was originally open to radio, television and magazine representatives, as well as public relations and advertising men in Virginia. In addition, several political and business leaders were invited to join as associate members. Later, when membership went over 200, the board of directors allowed business and professional men outside the mass communications field to join. A story in July 1955 had membership at 250. Originally for men only, the club later provided members' wives with club privileges. The club charged thirty dollars for membership, plus annual dues of thirty dollars. One brochure mentioned that the Press Club of Virginia was the only social club in Richmond without a waiting list.

The club's first president and first vice-president were Richard W. Payne Jr. and John Daffron, respectively. Its first manager was Paul H. Graham, who resigned as Jefferson Hotel assistant manager to switch over to the Press Club. Described as a "jovial gentleman," Graham was known as "the little Paul Whiteman" because of his resemblance to a musician of that name. Graham and his own orchestra—Paul Graham and his Crackers—played successful engagements at nightclubs and private clubs along the eastern seaboard for several years. He made a career change from music to hotels in 1940 and ended up at The Jefferson in 1950.

A club brochure quoted a guest from Texas: "The Jefferson is almost the last place on the North American continent that still retains the charm of the Old South. It is still the evidence that gracious living is even now available to the traveler." A July 1964 story mentioned that the Press Club had moved from The Jefferson Hotel to the new Mark Monroe Motor Inn.

THE ENGINEERS' CLUB

The Engineers' Club was founded at the Sheraton in 1961 and moved to The Jefferson a few years later, taking the space left vacant when the Press Club moved out. In 1974, it was reported that the club had 405 members. To be considered, prospective members had to have degrees in engineering, architecture or a chemical field. The club manager in 1974 was Mrs. Frances Gregg Morris.

FADING FAST IN THE 1960s

From 1968 on, in relatively short order, the alcohol law, as well as the deteriorating condition of The Jefferson and the surrounding neighborhood, hastened declining club memberships. It wasn't long until they started closing, leaving the hotel with a lot of unoccupied space and a lot less income. Before 1968, club members overlooked the aged hotel's unrenovated conditions because they had to in order to entertain with cocktails. But after 1968, they didn't have to.

On January 28, 1969, Watkins and Suttle were notified that The Jefferson had made the prestigious Virginia Landmarks Register and was nominated for the National Register of Historical Places. Nice accolades and impressive framed awards on an office wall but not much in the way of being able to install a new roof or upgrade the plumbing system.

The hotel was fading fast, on the road to its end. Richmond attorney Bill Shields recalls the army using the hotel in 1968 as a holding station of sorts—putting him and other new enlistees up there on metal-frame army-regulation cots, four to a room. He, like many others, characterized the hotel at the time as pretty seedy.

Whatever the condition, the hotel was denying admittance to people it didn't find respectable, regardless of ability to pay, like Jimi Hendrix. Hendrix played the Mosque on August 20, 1968. Record promoter Ron Brandon was with Hendrix at The Jefferson when he tried to check in. Brandon had made the reservation for Hendrix ahead of time, but the hotel denied admittance to the future rock-and-roll legend. Hendrix did not seem surprised and did not get perturbed or angry. They simply went to another hotel in Richmond that night. The two shows Hendrix put on that night were only half filled.

Several private businesses continued to rent space at the hotel through the 1970s, as the drinking change did not affect their mission. The Garden Club of Virginia and the Richmond Junior League had headquarters at the hotel—the Junior League in a fifth-floor suite and the Garden Club in the Arcade, an area off the Franklin Street entrance. The Virginia Federation of Women's Clubs, the Virginia Symphony Orchestra, the Virginia Retail Merchants Association and the Virginia Highway Users Association also rented space.

At about this time, several senior employees made their departure. Charles E. Byrd retired in April 1969, after twenty years with The Jefferson. He proudly boasted that in all that time, he was late with only one meal, and that was because nine hundred people showed up an hour early for a banquet.

Douglas "Enos" Tow retired as head chef in 1973 and was replaced by Heinrich Sneider. With the exception of a one-year break in 1957, when he worked at Thalhimer's, Mr. Tow had been the directing chef at The Jefferson for twenty-three years. In February 1950, the *Richmond Times Dispatch* reported Tow's arrival to The Jefferson:

> *French cooking and Virginia spoonbread have gotten together at last. Appropriately enough, the famous old Hotel Jefferson here has brought them together in a happy combination of typical Southern cooking with the exotic sauces that distinguish French cuisine. This meeting and blending of two fine culinary traditions seems significant. You could even take it as a sort of thumbing-of-the-nose at some recent criticism of Southern cooking…Spoonbread appears nightly at dinner, along with such delicacies as hearts of artichoke with a vinaigrette sauce, and broiled bluefish with pimiento butter, and many more.*

According to the June 1953 issue of *Commonwealth Magazine*, Tow would get excited telling how his kitchen once served 1,050 dinners in two dining rooms in just twenty-two minutes. Years earlier, Tow had played end on the Coe College (in Cedar Rapids, Iowa) football team that beat Wisconsin in the late 1920s. I don't know anything about that game or the significance of it, but there must have been something about it because it was mentioned in Tow's obituary when he died in February 2000. A lieutenant in the U.S. Navy, Tow is buried at Arlington National Cemetery.

Thomas Herbert retired from the Rotunda Club in 1974 after fifteen years of service. Prior to that, he worked for twenty-seven years at the Occidental, where, according to a 1974 *Richmond News Leader* story, he recalled waiting on Eleanor Roosevelt in the early 1930s.

As for an idea of prices, a menu from June 1970 reveals that a Maine lobster cost $8.50; prime ribs, $5.45; and an Omelet Schinkel (artichokes, mushrooms, tarragon and ham), $3.00. At the 1975 Tobacco Festival, a broiled eight-ounce sirloin steak was $7.50, and The Jefferson Special (imperial deviled crab and Virginia ham) cost $5.50. The 1979 Christmas dinner set you back $9.75.

In 1974, Manager Oakes said that the hotel normally had about 25 to 200 of its 330 rooms filled at any given time. A piece of bad news, insidiously eating away at potential profits, was the concentrated shift from overnight guests to permanent residents. The trend had grown precipitously over the years, to the point that the *Times Dispatch* reported on it in September 1968. This shift signaled failure. Yes, permanent residents paid money and paid consistently, but overnight guests paid more. And permanent residents didn't demand that everything sparkle and be renovated to the newest standards. Overnight guests did.

VII

Residents

By 1974, eighty full-time residents, from twenty to eighty-eight years of age, lived at The Jefferson. They included retired schoolteachers, diplomats, historians, an entertainer and a retired army colonel. One resident recalled, "We got to know each other. It was unusually pleasant within the community of those living in the hotel. It's the best place in town for those of us who don't want to keep house. It's a lazy type of life." You could get a single room for $60 to $150 a month (the $60 room did not have a bath) or two rooms and a bath for $300.[5]

Miss Emilie Hanewinkle, "a spinster of considerable means" and a part-time resident of The Jefferson and a permanent resident of Italy, ended up in a legal tussle with state tax authorities. She had left Virginia decades earlier for Rome but made periodic trips back to Richmond, always staying at The Jefferson. The issue was determining her domicile—if Richmond, she owed the tax; if Rome, she did not. The court ruled in her favor, stating that her conduct and comments showed that she did not consider Richmond home any longer and did not want to make it her home. The court ruled, "She was a woman of independent thought and firm views with both the courage and capacity to express them." The case was concluded in 1940, two years after Miss Hanewinkle died. Her estate did not have to pay the taxes of $1,505.24.

---

5. Most of the information regarding hotel residents comes from a *Richmond Times Dispatch* story by Meredith B. Homer.

Back to the 1970s. Mrs. J. Lewis White had a two-room suite at The Jefferson. "It takes me out of myself," she said. "I look around and see people worse off than I am…people who need help. As you get older, you have to adapt." She moved into the hotel in 1962. "It has become home to me. I have found many friends here." She joined the Colony Club, "the perfect place to entertain." She sometimes fixed herself breakfast and then got back in bed, nostalgically pretending that the maid she used to have in Bedford had magically prepared it.

Resident Wallace S. Harwood had retired from the IRS after a thirty-three-year career as a senior manager. Mr. and Mrs. Robert Seward left a farm on Isle of Wright County and moved to the hotel in 1969. He had been a student at the University of Richmond from 1917 to 1921 and then spent forty-five years working for the Virginia Department of Workmen's Compensation. His wife, he said, is "like a flea, the way she gets around." They often ate two meals a day at the hotel and went out for the third.

Howard W. Hite retired from R.J. Reynolds Tobacco after forty-two years and moved to The Jefferson in 1960 after his wife died. He sold his house in the west end and moved to the hotel "to come in contact with a little life." Permanent residents sometimes teased him about being a ladies' man. When questioned about that, he said, "Now you're getting into my secrets." He preferred to talk about another hobby: genealogy.

Mrs. Elizabeth Lawrence-Dow used to live "in one of the historic places" along the Potomac River before moving to her new home at the hotel, which she characterized as a lovely suite. She sometimes traveled to England to do genealogy work. Another woman—who did not want to give her name—stated that she had called the hotel home for twenty-five years. She lived there because she was alone and didn't like to do housework.

Reverend John A. MacLean, who grew up near the hotel and later moved away, started gravitating back to Richmond as a college student in North Carolina. He came to the hotel for dances after UNC-UVA games; years later, in 1969, the retired minister and his wife moved into the hotel.

James Carpenter might have been considered a part-time resident. From 1965 to 1970, he came down from Washington and spent every weekend at the hotel, always the same room, with the bathroom down the hall, for four dollars a night. In 1987, when he moved to the Westminster-

Mrs. Snead, hotel resident, circa 1980. *Courtesy of Sue Dayton.*

Canterbury Retirement Center, the hotel offered him his old room back for a night at the old familiar price of four dollars.

Perhaps the most sensational resident turned out to be millionaire heiress Esther Wilson Price. "Despite her substantial personal wealth," wrote Ted Gup in a 1979 story, Mrs. Price, daughter of John T. Wilson and widow of lumber businessman Conrad L. Price, moved into "Richmond's aging Jefferson Hotel" in the mid-1960s after all her immediate relatives died. She lived at the hotel for about a decade before moving to Missouri. She died at age eighty-one in August 1978, outside St. James, Missouri, at the 250-acre Yahweh City religious commune of a seventy-nine-year-old cult leader named Joseph Jeffers. Jeffers had been arrested for conspiring to murder his thirty-seven-year-old wife after she hid $2.5 million of Yahweh funds so Jeffers could not use them for his planned 1980 campaign for president of the United States. Mrs. Price's body was sent back to Richmond for burial at River View Cemetery.

GETTY

In 1965, Elizabeth Rousch published *Getty*, a fictional children's book about a seven-year-old boy who lived at The Jefferson with his wealthy uncle. Rousch was born and raised in Madison, Indiana. By the time she published *Getty* in 1965, thirty-year-old Rousch had been living for about five years at The Jefferson.

Rousch taught in Richmond at Saint Michael's Episcopal Day School and Saint Christopher's Preparatory School. She asked one of her students, Miss Campbell David, a girl of about sixteen who had an interest in art, to do the drawings for the book. As an adult, Campbell went on to work in the graphic arts field. The uncle in the book was based on one of Rousch's friends at The Jefferson. David went on to do the illustrations for Rousch's next book, *Getty at the Homestead*.

Rousch continued living at the hotel until February 1971, when she married a Cincinnati eye surgeon. Rousch's stepson characterized her as very precise, well read and a big fan of college football. Here are some parts of *Getty* that refer to the hotel:

> *We live at the Jefferson Hotel in Richmond, Virginia. It isn't a really famous hotel, but it's a very nice hotel. It's big and old and has lots of places to explore. There are places to hide in it too. Everybody at the Jefferson is very nice to me. I love living at the Jefferson…My favorite place to play at the hotel is in the storage room. It is full of old trunks, boxes, statues, and furniture…The Jefferson prints menus and stationery in the basement…The hotel manager called me into his office the other day. He was very upset with me. My favorite thinking place is the stairway in the lobby…The men who run the drug store in the hotel let me help them. I dust the boxes and straighten the magazines. Sometimes they let me help dry the dishes. They give me ice cream and candy…I eat dinner on the mezzanine. It is a big balcony. From the balcony you can see everything that happens in the lobby. I love to eat on the mezzanine…Room service carts are fun to ride. I ride them along the corridors pretending I'm Ben Hur driving my chariot… Sometimes at night I sneak out of my room and ride the elevator with the night elevator operator. She lets me ride up and down for as long as I want. If you think a hotel is exciting during the day, you should ride the elevator at night. It is like being in a different world…Well, I guess you can see I really love living at the Jefferson. I wish you could visit me.*

Elizabeth Rousch and Campbell David, author and artist of the children's book *Getty*.
Courtesy of Campbell David.

HORACE GANS

Any analysis of Jefferson residents begins with and ends with Horace Gans. There was probably no person (who didn't own or work at the hotel) with a closer connection and thorough knowledge of the hotel. When evicted in August 1980, the eighty-seven-year-old Gans had lived there for nearly four decades. When Gans moved into the hotel in 1941, there were more than one hundred permanent residents.

Gans was born a block away from the hotel. He remembered the fire of 1901 and was in the hotel on the night of the 1944 fire. He knew the very early years and the more recent ones, the best of times for the hotel and the not so good. He recalled the old days when there were public bathrooms for men and women at opposite ends of each floor. He vividly recalled The Jefferson's heyday, when it had "dances in the Palm Court with elaborate scenery—Arabian bazaars, igloos, log cabins surrounded by potted palm trees and covered by fake snow." Stained-glass windows were not removed during World War II, as many believe, because of the blackouts, Gans explained. They were removed because the hotel feared soldiers would throw bottles and break things. Gans said his favorite dish at The Jefferson was Lobster Thermidor—lobster served under glass with truffles, an edible fungus from France.

It was reported in October 1979 that there were about forty residents left, most retired and living alone. The number was split about evenly between men and women. By May 1980, according to the *Richmond News Leader*, there were only eight office tenants and twenty-six residents left. Monthly rates were $225 to $300 for bedroom and living room suites; nightly rates were $17 for a single and $22 for a double room. Manager Oakes wrote optimistically in a letter on July 30, 1980, that the hotel would close for renovations on August 31, with two years expected before reopening. The hotel was a financial wreck, weeks from closing, but the letterhead boasted, "Elegance You Can Afford" and "The Grandeur, Warmth and Traditions of Old Richmond—the Comforts of Today." Only about fifty employees were still on the hotel's payroll.

At the end of the 1970s, Sue Dayton, a student getting her bachelor's degree in Communication Arts and Design at Virginia Commonwealth University, worked as a hostess at the hotel. She became close with many of the residents. With their consent, she began taking portraits of her resident—friends using a Yashica LM square format camera. In 1980, in a show entitled "The Hotel Jefferson" at Richmond's Virginia Museum of Contemporary Art, she exhibited a collection of fifty photographs of the hotel and some of its residents and employees. Good thing for us that she put those interests and skills to work! With these pictures, you're looking straight into the tired eyes of the grand old dame and the people who called it home.

John Edmonds, hotel employee, 1980. *Courtesy of Sue Dayton.*

One of the photos shows John Edmonds, who at the time worked holidays and summers handling auditing duties. Edmonds was an English major at VCU. Thirty years later, Edmonds still recalls many of the hotel residents and employees. He said that former manager Dewitt Oakes was an old-school hotelier, a jovial man who had been stationed in the navy at Pearl Harbor on the Day of Infamy in 1941. Edwards recently wrote a book (*Where Scarlett Never Fell*) containing fictional short essays of hotel characters, including Pompey.

SHARP DECLINE

In 1980, hotel waitress Alice Davis and restaurant manager Amerigo Picchi, like all employees, were worried about the future of the hotel. They didn't know anything more than what they read in the papers. Ethel Wyne, the telephone operator for twenty-nine years, was also left to wonder. No one was telling Manager Oakes anything. Uncertainty spread among employees, and many headed for the doors looking for other jobs in the expectation that the hotel would soon close. Management made a concerted effort to convince employees to stay "and see what happens." One story in May 1975 reported that the owners had a minimum asking price of $3 million. Another story reported that the entire purchase/renovation could run as high as $10 million, a figure that turned out to be shockingly low.

Watkins and Suttle were offered about $3 million for the hotel by the Federal Reserve Bank of Richmond, which planned to replace it with a fifteen-story office building. Watkins was adamantly against selling to the Fed because he wanted the hotel saved, partly because of its historic nature but also because he liked using it as a home away from home on his frequent trips to Richmond, for business and pleasure.

There were several near-purchases of the hotel in the mid- to late 1970s, once real possibilities with lawyers and lengthy contracts, now just odd occurrences from yellowed newspaper articles. In the mid-1970s, a potential investment group came along, calling itself the Alligator Corporation, a clever play on the most famous guest and icon. Joseph Stettinius led this group and took out a fifteen-month option to determine whether it was economically feasible to buy and restore the hotel. Even with many of its rooms vacant, Stettinius said that the hotel showed a slight profit.

In October 1979, the U.S. Department of Housing and Urban Development (HUD) tried to buy it. It awarded $4.3 million to refurbish the hotel. In April 1980, the Richmond City Council approved the HUD grant to renovate The Jefferson. A few months later, however, a judge ruled that the grant to lend federal money to private developers was against the Virginia constitution. In March 1980, it was reported that Robert Coles Jr., president of the First Jefferson Corporation, said he expected to buy the hotel and invest $20 million to restore it. He thought he could reopen it by December 1981.

Suttle and Watkins made it abundantly clear that they were not going to pay for significant repairs. The manager of the Colony Club had to get her husband to clip the bushes and cut the grass in front of the hotel. Other problems effected comfort and safety, not just appearance. A section of a ceiling fell in the restaurant, and the boiler broke down, forcing guests to keep their jackets on. Eventually, someone from the Engineers' Club got the boiler fixed (they were engineers, after all), and the club deducted the cost from its rent. To be fair, the owners did occasionally put money into the hotel, just not enough. A 1974 story quoted Watkins as saying that he had spent $2 million in the prior two years for air-conditioning, two elevators, a new laundry room and a complete renovation of the kitchen. Often, however, money spent was not for improvements or renovations but simply to bring the hotel to a required legal standard. In May 1975, The Jefferson installed a new warning device in its heating system, an expense incurred to stave off further penalties. Neighbors had been complaining, and the hotel got fined for polluting the air. It wasn't hard to see that running this grand hotel on a petite budget would go only so far. The long-ignored hotel was in serious disrepair; decades of neglect had taken their toll. A tremendous amount of time, money and effort were required to keep and renovate the grand dame of the South to its former splendor.

Watkins put on a happy face during this difficult time, claiming that a 1974 advertisement in *Southern Living* magazine brought in as many as thirty inquiries a day. Management boasted that The Jefferson was one of only two hotels in America designated as a National Historic Landmark. According to a *Times Dispatch* story, many visitors were expected in mid-November 1976 as a result of NBC having just aired *Gone With the Wind*. The story of the hotel's Grand Staircase being connected to the staircase in the famous movie is apocryphal and legendary. The staircases in *Gone With the Wind* and The Jefferson Hotel are not connected. But the myth continues, and many Richmonders love to believe that maybe, just maybe, there might be some truth to it.

As for movies and cameras, The Jefferson and its Grand Staircase got filmed for an epic commercial that apparently was never shown. Rogers Rudd, the hotel's director of marketing, was quoted in a 1976 story as saying that the Gwaltney Meat Company filmed a commercial on The Jefferson staircase with 150 costumed actors. Rudd thought the commercial never aired. Gibson Worsham said the filming took pretty much an entire day and was open to anyone who showed up in a costume. The commercial for this meat company turned Clark Gable's famous line into something to the effect of: "Damn it, I don't give a frankly."

Things were on a hard decline, each sharp decision cutting away hope, or rather the delusion, of a turnaround. In January 1975, the hotel brought in William E. Hood as manager. Some people have a reputation that stalks them like a disease. In Mr. Hood, the ailing patient was getting a house call from Dr. Death. Anyone who cared about the hotel felt pessimism in the extreme. Hood might as well have been wearing a black hood over his head. He was a closer; that is, when he showed up, hotels closed down. A *Richmond Mercury* story reported that Hood had closed three of the last four hotels he'd managed, no doubt causing panic and worry for local preservationists. "If a place isn't going to make it economically," Hood proclaimed, "then I'm going to close it down. I don't do it for pleasure, but a business is a business." Temporarily putting his scythe down, the grim manager added that he thought The Jefferson would make it. "The way this hotel can make money is to concentrate on its history and its reputation…The Jefferson already has the basic facilities to be a great convention hotel, and a refurbished Jefferson could be a great drawing card. This place can work, and I'd like to see it start moving."

He estimated that it would take $10 million to purchase and renovate the hotel. The actual price to restore the hotel turned out to be $33 million, and that doesn't include the money to buy it. Everything was going poorly. Even the manager looked bad. DeWitt Oakes, who had temporarily stepped aside during William Hood's brief tenure as manager, suffered a stroke but continued working on a wing off the lobby. Bleak. Bleak. Everything looked bleak. The economy made it even worse.

The horrendous national economic crisis of the late 1970s was the death knell for any chance of a successful turnaround. After owning the hotel for three decades, Suttle and Watkins clung to the hope that they would be able to work something out. Perhaps they could weather the storm; after all, Suttle had started selling cars in 1931—very early in the Depression. He made it through the 1930s and was still selling them almost half a century later.

Eventually, however, the grim realization was inescapable: they had a toxic asset that they couldn't afford to keep and couldn't afford to renovate. They needed to make or borrow a lot of money, perhaps tens of millions of dollars, a near-impossible order even in good economic times. But this was happening in a massive economic crisis, with staggering inflation, unemployment and interest rates. Interest rates to borrow money were 17 percent and higher, and that's not credit card interest, either. Inflation and unemployment skyrocketed to double digits.

There were many contributing factors, including the fuel shortages, when the oil cartels reduced the flow of exported oil, causing gas prices to spike. Angry motorists fumed in long lines, and many cities went to specified approved gas purchase days. The fuel shortages, in turn, caused people to conserve gas money, and the way to do that was to buy one of the freshly imported Japanese vehicles. Most Americans saw fuel-sipping Datsuns, Hondas and Toyotas for the very first time. Japanese carmakers got a foothold in the American market in a radically fast and big way. Radio stations—mostly in Rust Belt states deeply affected by the imports—charged a dollar to take a whack with a sledgehammer at a foreign car. You didn't want to drive in a foreign car anywhere near Detroit, Pittsburgh or Cleveland—cities closely tied to the auto industry—in the late 1970s. Detroit had missed the boat and was still making massive, heavy, gas-guzzling land yachts that weren't selling, leaving thousands of people with jobs related to the assembly, sale and repair of American automobiles out of work. Trying to sell Fords and Chevys in the 1970s was like trying to stay in a lane after it merges into another. That other lane carried zippy little Hondas, and they darted quickly.

But what does all this have to do with The Jefferson Hotel? A lot. The men who owned The Jefferson at that time were auto dealers trying to sell American cars. Simply put: because people weren't buying Chevrolets, Suttle and Watkins didn't make enough money to do hotel renovations. In fact, they were barely getting by in their car businesses. Not only were Watkins and Suttle not earning money from the cars, but they were also actually losing money. Cars cost dealers money while they sit on a lot.

Suttle had to borrow money from his car dealerships, a transaction that put him at odds with the IRS. He considered the loan interest free, but the IRS disagreed and thought it was an attempt to avoid paying taxes. The IRS assessed additional taxable income of more than $17,000 for 1972 and 1973. Several years later, in October 1978, the tax court overruled the IRS and determined that the loans, from Suttle to himself, did not represent taxable income.

Money was too costly to borrow, even if they could find a lender. Watkins and Suttle, after all, were not bankers or developers, and they didn't even live or work in Richmond. They couldn't get the money, nor did they even have the time to make the effort that would have been required. These were, as described earlier, intensely busy men, with many activities going on. Renovating and saving The Jefferson at this crisis point was not a hobby or something one dabbled with.

So, the unsold cars collected dust. The idea of getting loans was a nonstarter. Hotel renovations and upkeep got ignored. Whatever work that was done got completed on a ludicrously minimal budget. No viable scenario would prevent our old fighter from going down for good. Had Watkins and Suttle owned a six-room motel along Route 1, they would have been able to keep it spruced up nicely, but The Jefferson was just too big and too old and too costly for the minuscule profits from selling gas-guzzling Chevy Impalas.

1980: THE END OF AN ERA

On Saturday, April 26, 1980, Nancy Jones of Ruther Glen, Virginia, married John Albright of Richmond, bestowing on them not only wedded bliss (they're still married) but also the possible title of the last couple to wed before the hotel closed in 1980, just the thing needed to turn any wedding scrapbook from good to great. A photograph of them getting married on the stairs is at the hotel's museum today. The new couple did not stay overnight, so they only saw the hotel's public areas. The Rotunda and the Grand Staircase were still closed off from The Jefferson Palm Court, the wall erected by the closed-up Rotunda Club having never been removed. The Albrights won the wedding package offered by a Richmond public radio station as part of a fund drive. Mrs. Albright recalls that the hotel was operating at the time like any other hotel; it still had employees and the capability to handle the reception had the new couple wanted it. Perhaps her view was simply that of seeing things through the enthusiastic lens of a wedding ceremony. Others described things a lot more harshly, often using the word "seedy." A little later, Eda Carter Williams recalled the following about the hotel:

> *As I walked through the shabby Main Street entrance (the front doors had long since been boarded up) and walked across the unswept marble floor, a deep sense of gloom swept over me. The black chairs were sagging in the deserted lobby, and the proud columns seemed too tired to hold up the building. There was no one at the desk, but a sloppy woman took us to the second floor in the rickety elevator.*

Horace Gans, who was finally evicted in August 1980, said:

> *It got to the point where they were losing money on the operation. The owners were not hotel people. They were not inclined to spend money. In the last year or so, drunks and drug peddlers and just about everything indecent and unwanted got in there; it really got down to the dregs.*

Tom Henley, who had been with Jefferson for about thirty years, recalled that the few remaining employees kept getting calls asking about room availability. By September 1980, everyone but DeWitt Oakes had left the building. "The tourists have heard about the hotel's reputation," Oakes reported, "but not its current condition." Finally, with drunks, drug dealers and dregs knocking at the door, the owners locked it up.

After it closed, a couple film crews descended on the hotel, using the enormous (and cheap) space of the vacant old Jefferson. In December 1980, director Louis Malle filmed *My Dinner with Andre*, a critically acclaimed artsy movie about two guys having an extended dinner conversation. There was no mention of The Jefferson in the movie, and you can't even tell it was filmed at the hotel. In fact, the dinner itself was supposed to have taken place in a New York City restaurant. The filming occurred over two weeks—two very cold weeks inside the hotel. According to the Internet Movie Database (IMDb) website, the $500,000 budget did not provide enough money to heat the hotel (The

Jefferson boilers weren't working), so the crew wore ski clothes, and the actors had to simply act warm, with only lights and long underwear to help out. "A bit of cognac" helped one producer deal with the cold. Released in October 1981, it's the New York Yankees of movies: you either loved it or hated it.

ROCK 'N' ROLL HOTEL

A movie filmed at The Jefferson in late 1982—*Rock 'n' Roll Hotel*—was simply one of the worst ever. Dale Brumfield detailed the filming and history of the movie in *Style Weekly*, noting that The Jefferson at the time was "a ghostly victim of urban flight and home to a handful of transients." The producers chose Richmond largely because of the film-friendly tax credits. At The Jefferson, they had plenty of space to set up various settings. One person involved with the project said that The Jefferson was "a big empty playground." Another—who clearly never read *Getty*—reported that he "roamed the dark and empty hotel like Eloise, the little girl in the famous kids' book." Judd Nelson was in it, before he became famous for *The Breakfast Club*. *Rock 'n' Roll Hotel* did have a memorable line: "Yes, Virginia, there is a Rock 'n' Roll Hotel." The movie was publicly shown one time in New York in 1983. No one saw it again until August 31, 2010, when it was shown at Richmond's Byrd Theatre. I made a point to see it.

The Jefferson Hotel hosted the pre-screening VIP party, a delightfully well-attended affair with all kinds of people who had some connection to the movie, including many who were filmed as extras. They all said the Rotunda looked very much like it did back when the hotel closed in 1980. The doors of the upstairs guest rooms back then were painted all styles and colors. One partier told me that he and Judd Nelson used to scurry around the hotel looking for cool nooks and crannies, like kids exploring a big house for the first time. None of the "stars" of the movie were at the party.

Mary Stuart Cruickshank and Cecilia Brooks joined me at the party and the movie. They had both worked at the hotel a few years earlier, and Mary Stuart is rightfully often referred to as the hotel historian. After the party, we made the bus ride to the Byrd. The entire event was a fundraiser to save the historic theater. Our VIP tickets got us fine seats up in the mezzanine. When it took an inordinately long time to get the movie started, one clever wit shouted, "It took twenty-eight years to get this far, hopefully it won't be another twenty-eight!" Everyone chuckled. To get every last laugh, he said it again. I bought the ultimate souvenir: a T-shirt with the clever "Give Richmond the Byrd" slogan. We moviegoers had been sufficiently warned by Brumfield to expect a really bad movie. But you hear that about many movies. This was different. With bad acting, a bad script, a bad plot and bad dialogue, it was no-kidding *bad*. Scenes mysteriously cut off, and scenes suddenly appeared. We went back to The Jefferson, where Mary Stuart, Cecilia and I nightcapped on desserts and Bailey's Irish coffee. Great company, delectable treats, a good cause and a terrible movie: three out of four isn't bad.

VIII

The Purchase

In 1983, when George Ross and his partners—Frank Weber and Richard (Richie) Siegel—dangled $3.4 million in front of Suttle and Watkins for their old boarded-up building, it was too good to pass up. When the purchase was reported, Richmond columnist Steve Clark called The Jefferson "a decayed reminder of something that once was very fine…[It] has become an eyesore on the city's skyline." Ross, Weber and Siegel formed RWS Associates in June 1982. They were general partners with 25 percent ownership each; the remaining 25 percent was evenly split between the musician Billy Joel and his former wife.

Ross said it was the most complex transaction he has ever been involved in, and in half a century as a developer, he's done a lot of deals. It surely fattened a lot of lawyers' bank accounts. At one point during the transaction, Ross counted some twenty-seven different lawyers involved.

During this period, you may have seen in the Richmond area one of the ten thousand red-and-white bumper stickers to "Save The Jefferson." With fees and taxes, RWS Associates bought the hotel on May 9, 1983, for cash and promissory notes totaling precisely $3,645,707.45, with cash due from the purchaser at settlement of $615,707.45. A couple of months later, the property conveyed from RWS Associates to Jefferson Hotel Associates Ltd. The deed was recorded on November 2, 1983.

There were many commendations sent to the new owners. A letter to the editor by a Robert Grant Willis of Richmond included:

Bumper sticker. *Courtesy of George Ross.*

> *Richmonders should rejoice at the announcement that finally the Hotel Jefferson has come into the hands of tasteful, creative businessmen who will restore this extraordinary building to its former stateliness, for the decaying edifice on Franklin Street is no ordinary hotel...The Jefferson means many different things to as many different people... During a quieter more refined era before television, moving pictures, and the motor car, generations of Richmonders simply walked to The Jefferson just to behold its grandeur. The hotel had become the hub of social, political and romantic activity in Richmond. The very name was synonymous with all that was par excellence.*

In a letter in 1983, the ninety-one-year-old Horace Gans thanked Ross for undertaking the project to save The Jefferson and added that he (Gans) "only hope that I can live long enough to see you make it better."

GEORGE ROSS

In a *Style Weekly* story, Carol O'Connor Wolf called Ross "Richmond's own Prince Charming," a perfect description of someone who would venture to buy the grand old dame in the economic crisis of the early 1980s. One columnist incorrectly reported that Ross was a Richmond native who went to dances at The Jefferson in his younger days. Ross never lived in Richmond as a youngster and never went to dances at the hotel.

In 1964, he completed his first project—an eighteen-story building at Eighth and Main, the first office building built in Richmond in forty years. His dad, who had built Holiday Inns and operated restaurants, brought George into the business.

The Purchase

Perhaps the most important thing to know about Ross is something you won't find in any biographical sketch. He's modest, unpretentious and down to earth. When I first contacted him to request an interview, there was no hesitation, no wondering if his interests would be covered or spun a certain way. No lawyers, no ground rules, no restrictions. He welcomed me into his office, showed me his collection of memorabilia from The Jefferson and offered to let me take anything and borrow it. He made his copier and office open to me whenever I wanted to stop by. His office is adorned with several mementos of The Jefferson Hotel, including a framed photograph and the commemorative coin from the reopening in May 1986.

Historic tax credits—state and federal—made the project doable and financially viable. The group originally formed to buy the hotel consisted of about a dozen people, including Jack Nicholas and Oscar Meyer, but most of these investors did not stay on.

George Ross, the man who saved The Jefferson. *Courtesy of George Ross.*

During the renovation, Ross was quoted as saying what everyone who knows the hotel knows: "The Jefferson has probably touched every family in the Richmond area for many, many years at some point in their lives." He made a point to use or donate whatever could be salvaged. To the Edgar Allan Poe Museum, he gave the shrubbery from the house next door at Franklin and Adams, where the porte-cochère was built. The Virginia Museum of Fine Arts received a five-foot bronze statue of two Indian figures, which had been donated by George Arents in 1902. The Valentine Museum got original architect's blueprints. He could have taken this stuff home or sold it, and no one would have cared or noticed. After all, he and his partners owned the hotel.

Before the renovation got started, they had to get rid of much of the old, and they did that by bringing in the Valentine Auction Company. The contract with the auction company had twenty-two separate sections. Valentine collected 20 percent on the first $75,000 sold and 25 percent on everything over $75,000. The booklet described and numbered 2,296 different items to be auctioned over five days. On the first day—September 9, 1983—one thousand people showed up to bid on 240 items. Sales that day exceeded $20,000.

Tarrant's Restaurant at Foushee and Broad picked up marble slabs from The Jefferson. After a good cleaning, Tarrant's turned them into a restaurant counter, where your drink today would be perched if you sat at the bar. Bartender Danny Holcomb told me that the marble counter was bought for twenty dollars a slab from the hotel. At the hotel, it had been used in a vertical manner—as a stall in the men's bathroom. Ted Santarella, owner of Tarrant's, makes his way over, and before long he's showing me a notebook about the history of Tarrant's. Richmond truly is a historic city, and much of that history includes The Jefferson. It turns out, the land Tarrant's sits on was purchased by Peter H. Mayo in the mid-1880s and was owned by the Mayo family until 1959. Mayo was one of the directors of The Jefferson Hotel in 1905. Somehow, almost everything in Richmond seems to connect to The Jefferson.

In renovating the old hostelry, nothing was easy for Ross and his partners. Authorization to start work was muddled in contractual issues and bureaucracy. *Times Dispatch* reporter Jerry Lazarus stated that the deal allowing the renovation to go forward was as complex as the renovation work itself. Sybedon Corporation, a New York company, managed the financing and acted as primary partner for the overall deal, as well as the hotel's restoration. Algernon Blair of Montgomery,

Alabama, was hired as general contractor. It was the only company that would agree to a completion guarantee. Ross brought in an architect with whom he had previously worked, Vlastimil Koubek, of Washington, D.C. Manufacturers Hanover Trust, of New York, loaned the money. Once the hotel was rebuilt, it was sold to Prudential Bache. The investors then leased the hotel back. You no doubt noted the references to New York entities, an inescapably maddening frustration for Ross and his partners that they had to go outside Richmond to get the project done. Local bankers wouldn't loan any money—they didn't think it would work—primarily because a couple of new competing hotels were opening at the time in Richmond. City officials wouldn't loan anything, either, even for the sidewalk outside. Ross did end up, however, getting $128,100 in grant money through the city to move the hotel residents to other housing.

The 330 rooms were to be made into about 285 rooms and suites. Ross had heard about Carol Hochheiser, a designer who had done an impressive job on a tight budget at a couple of New Jersey hotels. Hochheiser and her partner Brad Elias had done interior design projects all over the world. Ross went to New Jersey, saw the work himself and decided to hire Hochheiser but was advised shortly afterward by Sheraton Corporation that he could not hire her because it had its own designers to make up the hotel the "Sheraton Way." Ross knew that John Kapioltas, then chairman of Sheraton International, was Greek by descent. Ross, who speaks fluent Greek, personally called Kapioltas and—in Greek—told Kapioltas that if he (Ross) couldn't hire his own designer, he would find another management company. The deal with Sheraton had not been finalized at that point. Kapioltas agreed, and The Jefferson hired the Hochheiser-Elias Group for $350,000, a decision everyone seemed happy with at the end.

Renovation plans went into action on June 27, 1985, when the Sheraton hosted a grand reception, with five hundred in attendance. Invitations stated: "In honor of the renovation and reconstruction of the historic Jefferson Hotel as we build a new beginning on the foundations of an illustrious past."

Once the work started, it went quickly. To make sure things got done right, Ross lived in the Governors Suite for a month and a half. It wasn't much at the time, but at least it had a balcony (otherwise known as loggia in architectural jargon). Some 350 workers swarmed the hotel, pouring $33 million into the old wreck, turning it back into a first-class hotel.

View from the northeast. *Courtesy of The Jefferson Hotel.*

A *Mid-Atlantic Country Magazine* story described the plasterwork done by C. Minor Stowe of Richmond, who learned the craft in his family; his father, grandfather and two uncles were plasterers. He had trouble finding anyone with the skill to help, so he did the work with just one young apprentice. He felt gratified to see people interested in his workmanship, especially those "who have something to do with the Historical Society." The story spelled out the process:

> *When a piece of ornamental plaster is so damaged that it can't be repaired, Stowe restores it by making a cast of another complete ornament. He begins by painting a liquid rubber on the ornament, taking about five to six days to add ten coats of the substance. He then pours casting plaster over the rubbery layer, lets it dry and uses the resulting mold to create a new but authentic plaster ornament. The work is time consuming—and attention grabbing.*

Thomas Jefferson Statue. *Courtesy Special Collections and Archives, James Branch Cabell Library, Virginia Commonwealth University Libraries.*

The Thomas Jefferson Statue had to be turned toward the east to greet guests coming in from the new entrance. To move the direction of the statue, Ross had to get permission from the Virginia Department of Historic Resources. For fear of damaging the statue, the contractor turned only the top part, leaving the base as it was originally positioned—facing Franklin Street. Several writers over the years have incorrectly reported that the statue originally faced south, toward Main Street. If you look at the base and the inscriptions on all sides, you will see that Jefferson's name is on only one side—certainly that would be the front, and that side faces north, toward Franklin Street. In addition, the *Richmond Dispatch* reported on October 27, 1895—a few days before the hotel originally opened—that the statue faced the Franklin Street entrance.

To get the 25 percent tax credit for cleaning historic bricks, specific Department of the Interior rules had to be followed. The bricks had to be cleaned chemically and then washed with pressure steam. They could not be sand blasted. Susceptible to erosion and deterioration, the brick was "like a loaf of bread in which removal of the hard outer crust of the old brick exposes the soft inner clay."

They tried to bring the alligators back but couldn't get permission. They even considered obtaining the rights to bottle and sell Jefferson Hotel spring water, and this was before anyone bought or sold water by the bottle.

1986 REOPENING

To show off the restored Jefferson, the Sheraton hosted a black tie reception on January 25, 1986, featuring the Gene Donati Orchestra. When the "soft" opening occurred on Saturday, March 15, only 125 of the 276 guest rooms and suites were ready. Single rooms went for $85; double rooms, $99; and executive suites, $100 per day. An advertisement proclaimed, "A place where presidents presided, dignitaries dined, and alligators ruled the lobby." The Virginia Association of Museums held its annual meeting at The Jefferson Sheraton Hotel on March 20–22, 1986. On May 5, 1986, after a $33 million renovation, the nearly unimaginable happened. The old edifice, having miraculously dodged the wrecking ball, was not a towering office building or a barren parking lot. It was once again The Jefferson Hotel, proud and stately. Perhaps somebody put a flower that day at Lewis Ginter's mausoleum in

Hollywood Cemetery or made a toast to the memory of Joseph Bryan. The full-page advertisement proclaimed: "Today, a Grand Tradition Returns to Richmond...So once again witty women and charming men will sip cordials by the alligator pond in the Palm Court."

At the opening ceremony, the Russell Wilson Quartet—with piano, bass and two flutes—performed music from the baroque era. Horace Gans made it. The former resident announced, "The old Jefferson, that had the best of everything in its proud days, is back." (Gans went on to visit the hotel for several more years; he was back for an event in 1995 at the age of 103.) Aptly dressed in a Jeffersonian-era costume was Robert Coles, the five-times great-grandson of Thomas Jefferson.

Along with champagne, some appropriate remarks were uttered. Hotel marketing director Susan Epps-Marstiller opined: "Never has a hotel captured the pulse of a people—of a city—as The Jefferson Hotel has." Sheraton chairman John Kapioltas said, "A hotel of this nature matures, but never ages." The Sheraton opened a new modern hotel every eight days, he reported, but the chances "to duplicate a concept of this nature...are very few, very rare." Another Sheraton executive said what everyone knew and felt: "We have five years of blood, sweat and tears in this project. We give a damn about it."

George Ross and Manager Hans Jasper, 1986. *Courtesy of George Ross.*

Margaret Ferguson, a Jefferson accountant from 1961 to 1975 was there, as was Alice Davis, a waitress for four decades. George Ross, the man who saved the hotel, proclaimed: "You can stay in an ultra-modern hotel in any major city in the world, but there is only one Jefferson." Shortly before opening, Ross got a congratulatory phone call from a man who said he was one of the original partners of the architectural firm that designed the hotel.

To break even, the hotel needed to be occupied 75 percent of the time at an average room rate of about seventy dollars. The nearby Marriott, which had recently opened, was charging about fifty dollars. The nearby John Marshall Hotel was still in business, but barely. It would close down in 1988. First to use the grand ballroom after the reopening was the Founders Dinner of Hampden-Sydney College, where about 375 people dined and danced to the music of the Kings of Swing.

In June 1987, NBC filmed a four-hour miniseries in Richmond called *The Ballad of Mary Phagan*. Scenes were filmed at various locations, including The Jefferson Hotel. Governor Baliles even had a speaking role: "Sir, I'm from Virginia, and I protest." Starring Jack Lemmon, the movie was about a murder that occurred in Atlanta in 1913. George Stevens, the film's producer selected Richmond for filming because Atlanta had been "paved over," and he thought Virginia was a much more restoration-conscious state.

In November 1988, Charles Kuralt did his nationally televised Sunday morning road show from The Jefferson. He started the segment by saying that you could tell a lot about a country by the buildings it builds, but "a country's character is also illuminated by the buildings it saves." The Jefferson Hotel, "again the pride of the South," looked "like a painting by Vermeer." Its public rooms, Kuralt opined, "are the most beautiful of any in the country." He called the hotel a "glowing reflection of the gilded age," with architecture "part Villa Medici, part Tower of Seville and part French chateau."

The Virginia Society, Sons of the American Revolution, declared its 100th annual conference in February 1989. With the exception of the years 1980 through 1986 (when the hotel was closed), the group held all its annual meetings at The Jefferson. Its first meeting at the hotel in 1896 was the group's seventh annual meeting.

FRANK SINATRA

In March 1994, Frank Sinatra played the Mosque for two nights; the crooner and his entourage stayed at The Jefferson. Sinatra commented several times about how much he loved the hotel, especially the Rotunda and the upper lobby. At the hotel after the concert the first night, pianist Anthony Dowd and saxophonist Skip Gailes entertained Sinatra and his entourage of nine or ten friends. The seventy-eight-year-old Sinatra even sang a couple tunes. Sinatra's meal began with a classical antipasto of marinated portobello mushrooms and Italian meats, cheeses and sausages, followed by baked focaccia, medium-rare Chateaubriand steak and a bouquetiere of vegetables. All this was topped off with New York–style cheesecake and chocolate Grammy cake created by Jefferson pastry chef Michael Martins.

With sales tax added in, the hotel bill for Sinatra's group was $19,819.50, which included forty-six rooms for three nights, each at $100, and nine luxury suites. Sinatra's room—Suite 156—cost $725 per night and came stocked with (based on his request) Special K cereal, bran flakes, bananas, oranges, whole milk, skim milk, Tabasco sauce, English muffins, crackers, six cans of Bumble Bee Tuna Fish, peanut butter, jams, honey, Aunt Jemima pancake mix, one dozen eggs, bacon, Grey Poupon mustard, butter, mocha mix, three cans Campbell's pork and beans, a toaster, tortilla chips, coffee (regular and decaf), celery, tomatoes, carrots, onions, thin-sliced Italian bread, olive oil, Lipton tea bags, four whole grapefruits and Bloody Mary mix.

Things did not go well for Sinatra on the second night. He collapsed onstage midway through "My Way." But the orchestra, according to a biography by Barbara Sinatra, "gamely played on." Immediately after getting checked at the hospital, Sinatra got on a plane and left town that night.

CHANGE IN OWNERSHIP

By the summer of 1989, Richmonders read two disparate stories about the hotel. The good news was that it was one of thirty-two charter members of the Historic Hotels of America (HHA), a commendation for meeting standards set by the National Trust for Historic Preservation. The bad news was that it had serious financial problems. In September 1989, the

Sheraton-Jefferson was facing foreclosure. With $292,000 owed in personal property taxes and $118,000 in real estate taxes, the hotel was the largest tax debtor in Richmond. In addition, the architect had sued for more than $113,000. The Jefferson Hotel Associates filed for Chapter 11 and vowed to stay open through the bankruptcy. The hotel and surrounding land were assessed at $17.3 million, a little more than half the cost of the renovation from a few years earlier. Hotel business was excellent; in fact, business was up 15 percent from the prior year. An auction was held to raise the $113,000 to pay the architect, but in September 1990, the Virginia Supreme Court nullified the auction of hotel fixtures, the Thomas Jefferson Statue and two Yamaha grand pianos. The court ruled that the auction was not carried out in a manner to attract multiple bidders, thereby preventing the auctioneer from obtaining the highest possible price.

Manufacturers Hanover Bank took possession of the hotel in accordance with a reorganization plan approved by the U.S. Bankruptcy Court in New York. A new group took over, and the grand old hotel opened again—for the fourth time—on November 6, 1991. Live alligators were brought in for the celebration. In quick order, a $3 million renovation project commenced.

Hotel life continued, and music, as always, played a significant role. In April 1992, the hotel hosted regular jazz ensembles to showcase local musicians, including Skip Gailes (often referred to as the "house musician"), Glenn Wilson, Brett Young and pianists Debo Dabney and Steve Kessler. In 1992–93, the hotel held a big band series, featuring acts like the Jimmy Black Quintet, Walt Howell Sextet, the Bruce Swartz Group and the Tommy Whitten Quintet.

On April 13, 1993, the hotel hosted a "Dinner with the President" party to celebrate Thomas Jefferson's 250th birthday. Partiers feasted on escargots on grilled polenta; catfish soup with sunchokes, truffles and roast leeks; and roasted lamb loin wrapped in wild mushroom confit, herbs and Virginia bourbon glaze.

In November 1993, big business arrived when *Fortune* magazine hosted its Fortune 500 Forum. At the time, the metro Richmond area was home to thirteen of the five hundred Fortune businesses. Brian Mott, a VCU public relations member, was one of about 150 Richmonders who volunteered to chauffeur a Lincoln town car for the likes of Mikhail Gorbachev. The business executives were smitten with The Jefferson. Herbert Kelleher, president of Southwest Airlines, was quoted as saying, "This hotel is magnificent. I wish I could take it home with me."

Painting of the Grand Staircase. *Courtesy of Parks Pegram Duffey III.*

In November 1994, Dr. Fillmer Hevener of Farmville, Virginia, exhibited his paintings at what was then called the Jaspers Parlor Gallery, near the Grand Staircase. The collection included paintings of Thomas Jefferson, John F. Kennedy and Booker T. Washington.

THE CENTENNIAL ANNIVERSARY

The Jefferson Hotel turned one hundred on October 31, 1995. To celebrate, it hosted a party billed as "The Party of the Century." The Jimmy Black Orchestra performed, as did the Richmond Pops Band and the Skip Gailes Ensemble. Proceeds benefited the Children's Hospital.

The hotel commissioned Parks Pegram Duffey III, a lifetime Richmonder, to draw festive Jefferson Hotel icons and images into one painting. His works were exhibited at the hotel and can be purchased today at the hotel's gift shop. Duffey also painted two other hotel scenes: an exterior view from Franklin Street and the Grand Staircase. He paints mostly historic buildings and events, including the Old Post Office and Pavilion in Washington, D.C.

Hotel management established an exhibit area in the northeast corner of the Rotunda, in space occupied for many years by the writing room. Pam Michael, with help from John Fralin and hotel employee Mary Stuart Cruickshank, reached out to everyone she could think of to gather mementos from the first century. People went through their old files and found documents, photos and souvenirs. There's the front page of the newspaper after the 1901 fire, a photograph from the 1932 Beaux-Arts Ball, guest folios and the program from the 1927 Lindbergh dinner, with a letter about how little Tommy Murrell Jr. camped out during the event at Lindbergh's feet. There's the newspaper story about "Tic-Toc" Allen Barringer in 1955 and a photo of perhaps the last wedding on the stairs before the hotel closed in 1980.

I believe the best description of the hotel comes from a book called *Southern Hospitality* by Emyl Jenkins:

> *The Jefferson Hotel in Richmond, Virginia is grand—but not too grand. She's the sort of…hotel where a string quartet plays during afternoon tea, but there isn't a white-gloved lady in sight. She is elegant, but relaxed, dignified but not stuffy. This is her heritage.*

Epilogue

It has been thoroughly enjoyable researching and writing this book. I got to know the hotel employees, especially those at the front desk and reception area. During the year I researched this book, The Jefferson really was my home away from home. James Winston (JW) would always greet me with a friendly face and tell me a few things about the hotel from the 1980s. At the concierge desk, Angela Kyle and Jeanita Harris would always greet me with: "Welcome home, Mr. Herbert." When I told them to call me Paul, they always reminded me that they weren't allowed to address hotel guests by first name. They are like air-traffic controllers, busily juggling calls, requests and questions thrown at them in waves yet always keeping friendly, professional demeanors. Then it was on to the registration desk, where, regardless of how long it had been since my prior visit, I was always welcomed by name by Patricia Coles and David Glover. Hotel management must send the employees to memory school to remember all the guests' names. I'd stop and chat with Greg Reinstaler and Greg Reed. The walk over to the coffee shop would always result in a pleasant conversation with Merdis Miller. At night, I'd hang out for a little while chatting with the night shift guys, Ben Corpus, Brent "the Kid" Hassard or Anthony "Tony the Greek" Kontoleon. Then it was into the bar for a beverage, served cold by Clint Southall, the bartender—a friendly, well-informed sports fan. They're all friendly folks at the hotel, and pardon the cliché, but I felt like family.

Alas, we get to the end of the hotel's first century. It survived fires, economic depressions and competing upscale hotels. It still stands proudly. Fortunately, people like Bettie Hobson, Fran Kizer and Sue Powell Williams assembled scrapbooks years ago; Sue Dayton and Jim Oliver took some remarkable pictures; and Jeanita Harris, George Ross and Leta McVeety preserved mementos and documents. Who knows what the next century holds: Who will be the Joseph Bryan or Al Suttle to rescue the maiden if she falls? Will there be another George Ross to ensure she doesn't get razed for an office building? Where will the Edwin Slipek Jr., Gibson Worshams and Michael Ajemians come from to eloquently share her rich history? For the sake of Richmond, for Virginia and for history, I hope they're out there and don't falter.

The Jefferson is the perfect combination of luxury and comfort. It's like a museum, but you're encouraged to relax and feel at home. It's a five-star luxury hotel, yet the rooms are affordable. Yes, the grand dame shows her age; yes, she's got a few wrinkles and gray hairs, but she's earned them. It's a fabulous hotel with two great restaurants. Make a point to go over there once in a while for dinner or drinks and encourage visitors to Richmond to stay there overnight. You'll have a great time. It's a fun place. I truly hope The Jefferson Hotel—Richmond's Grand Dame—lives forever. Long may she run.

Bibliography

ARTICLES

Allen, Mike. "Jefferson Sheraton Facing Foreclosure." *Richmond Times Dispatch*, September 22, 1989.

Alvey, Edward, Jr. "John F. Allen and Lewis Ginter: Richmond Cigarette Pioneers." *Richmond Literature and History Quarterly* 7 (Winter 1984).

Bayliss, Mary Lynn. "The Dooleys: A View from Their Library." *Richmond Literature and History Quarterly* 9 (Summer 1986).

Bien, William. "Hotelman's Happy at The Jefferson." *Richmond News Leader*, n.d.

———. "Official Resigns at Jefferson to Direct New Press Club." *Richmond News Leader*, October 16, 1953.

———. "100 Club Managers Reminisce about Nightmares at Meeting." *Richmond News Leader*, October 25, 1955.

———. "The Stately Jefferson Gets a New Look." *Commonwealth Magazine* (February 1955).

———. "Virginia's Newshawks Come to Roost." *Virginia and the Virginia County* (December 1953).

Brown, Alexander C. "Richmond's Famous Hotel Jefferson Well Maintained Reputation for Southern Hospitality." N.p., n.d.

Brumfield, Dale. "Yes, Virginia, There Is a "Rock 'n' Roll Hotel." *Style Weekly*, August 18, 2010.

Burtch, Susan T. "Once Upon a Time." *Richmond Magazine*, October 1974.

Calos, Katherine. "Jefferson Hotel: Return to Grandeur." *Richmond News Leader*, June 9, 1983.

Campbell, Tom. "Hotel Jefferson's Majesty Emerges as Dust Removed." *Richmond Times Dispatch*, n.d.

Clark, Steve. "At Long Last, The Jefferson Is Back—and It Is Something to See." *Richmond News Leader*, March 20, 1986.

Clinger, David. "Greek Orthodox Church Ordains Young Priest." *Richmond Times Dispatch*, October 14, 1957.

Crews, Ed. "Investors Buy Jefferson, Promise to Stress Local Ties." *Richmond Times Dispatch*, n.d.

Crosby, D. "Hotel Jefferson Again Set to Rise from Ashes after Years of Neglect." *Downtown Campus News*, February 1983.

Dunford, Earle. "Red Carpet Is Rolled Out for Reynolds Family." *Richmond Times Dispatch*, November 18, 1957.

Fair, Kathleen. "The Rotunda Club: A Chronicle of the Birth, Rise, and Demise of a Gentleman's Club." N.p., n.d.

Foster, William B. "Renovation Nearly Finished at Historic Jefferson Hotel." *Richmond News Leader*, August 7, 1952.

Friddell, Guy. "Defenders Will Hold Va. Convention Here." *Richmond News Leader*, March 1, 1957.

Geran, Monica. "Jefferson Sheraton Hotel, Richmond: The Rebirth of a Virginia Landmark with Interiors by Hochheiser-Elias Design Group." *Interior Design Magazine* (April 1987).

Grandis, Carolyn. "Designer's Grand Plans for The Jefferson Unfold." *Richmond Times Dispatch*, April 24, 1984.

Green, Barbara. "Five Stars: Restored Hotel Brings Elegance to Town." *Richmond News Leader*, June 27, 1984.

Hall, Larry. "Challenged to a Duel, He Vanquished a Custom." *Richmond Times Dispatch*, August 25, 2004.

———. "Yes, Mr. Gator, Your Room Is By—Well, in—the Pool." *Richmond Times Dispatch*, February 25, 2005.

Harper's Weekly. "The Jefferson of Richmond, Virginia." December 7, 1895.

Henley, Bernard J. "Richmond's Introduction to the Authomobile." *Richmond Literature and History Quarterly* 4 (Fall 1981).

Holiday, Ann. "Sandblasting Strips Dirt, Durability, Looks from Historic Bricks." *Richmond News Leader*, May 31, 1984.

———. "Warehouse Stores Treasures from Past of Hotel Jefferson." *Richmond News Leader*, August 7, 1985.

Hosts, S.H.A. "Cavalier-Jefferson Corp. Has Grown Steadily under Banks' Leadership." *Hotel World-Review*, July 14, 1956.

"Hotel Jefferson." *Commonwealth Magazine* (June 1953).

Howland, Richard Hubbard. "Echoes of a Gilded Epoch." *Arts in Virginia* (Fall 1964).

Jensen, Karen. "Keeper of a Lost Art." *Mid-Atlantic Country Magazine* (January 1986).

"John Jasper, Unique and Unforgettable." *Richmond Literature and History Quarterly* 1 (Summer 1978).

Kollatz, Harry, Jr. "Up to the Caberet: The Jefferson Hotel's Vaudeville Aerie." *Richmond Magazine*, July 2001.

Lang, M.C. "Let the Records Bark!" *Prologue Magazine* 43, no. 4 (Winter 2011). National Archives.

Lee, John. "Manufacturers Set Up Exhibit Booths at Hotel." *Richmond New Leader*, October 15, 1957.

Lemon, Conrad. "Hotel Would Recapture Bygone Grandeur." *Richmond Times Dispatch*, October 4, 1964.

Mericle, C. Dale. "Contractor Finds Solution to Tough Job." *Air Conditioning & Refrigeration News*, May 14, 1956.

Morris, Thomas R. "Ross Partnership Buys Jefferson Hotel." *Richmond Times Dispatch*, May 1983.

Moyer, Laura. "Memorabilia, Bargains Draw Crowd to Auction." *Richmond Times Dispatch*, September 11, 1983.

November, Neil. "I Remember When..." *Richmond Times Dispatch*. June 19, 1949.

Osborn, Maria. "Jefferson Acts to Chase Blues." *Richmond Times Dispatch*, October 22, 1989.

Pettinger, Betty. "Detailed Plans to Renovate Jefferson Hotel Outlined." *Richmond Times Dispatch*, September 1980.

———. "History Checks Out at Jefferson; Makes Reservation at Valentine." *Richmond Times Dispatch*, February 17, 1985.

Potter, Bruce. "Second Restoration for Hotel Is Praised." *Richmond News Leader*, n.d.

Proctor, Roy. "Vaudeville Played Jefferson Hotel Roof Garden in Hotel's Early Days." *Richmond News Leader*, March 5, 1988.

Richmond Mercury. "The Jefferson: A Second Chance for a Grand Hotel?" May 28, 1975.

Richmond News Leader. "Colony Club, Soon to Open, Names Mrs. Bender Manager." December 18, 1955.

———. Editorial. April 1, 1949.

———. "Hotel Was Home in Family Scrapbook." October 22, 1985.

————. "Low Calorie Elegance Asked by All-Woman Club Guests." December 26, 1968.

————. "New Club's Formation Eyed Here." June 8, 1949.

————. "Pythians Hold Business Session." October 7, 1957.

————. "Requests ABC Liquor License." N.d.

————. "Richmond in Bygone Days." October 25, 1955.

————. Souvenir magazine section. May 30, 1992.

————. "Va. Nurses Meet to Up Membership." September 24, 1957.

Richmond Times Dispatch. "State Angus Unit Makes Three Awards." N.d.

————. "*Toxicodendron Pubescens* Found in *Parthenocissus Quinquefolia.*" October 9, 1952.

Robertson, Dorothy. "The Mixing Bowl." *Richmond Times Dispatch,* February 8, 1950.

Rolfe, Shelley. "Jefferson Hotel Won't Be Just a Memory after Tomorrow." *Richmond Times Dispatch,* March 14, 1986.

————. "Ribbon-Cutting at The Jefferson." *Richmond Times Dispatch,* May 7, 1986.

Row, Steve. "Community Love Made Jefferson Project Work." *Richmond News Leader,* May 6, 1986.

Ruehlmann, William. "A Return to Splendor." *Virginia Pilot,* April 20, 1986.

Salmon, Emily J. "The Belle of the Nineties: Richmond's Jefferson Hotel, 1895–1995." *Virginia Cavalcade* 45 (Summer 1995).

Schreiner, Ray. "When Gators Roamed The Jefferson." N.p., n.d.

"The Seaboard Air Line." *Virginia Cavalcade* 33 (Spring 1984).

Slipek, Edwin, Jr. "Belle Epoch." *Style Weekly,* April 25, 1995.

————. "Nip, Tuck, Expand and Adorn." *Style Weekly,* August 8, 2000.

————. "A Perfect Union." *Style Weekly,* May 9, 1995.

Taylor, Joe. "Sir, I'm from Virginia." *Free Lance Star* [Fredericksburg, Virginia], June 5, 1987.

Valentine, Ross. "A Book about The Jefferson." *Richmond Times Dispatch,* January 15, 1965.

Virginia Magazine of History and Biography 96 (April 1988).

Virginia Pilot. "Bulk of Consolvo's $2 Million Is Willed to DePaul Hospital and St. Mary's Girl Orphanage." October 28, 1947.

Virginia Publisher & Printer. "Virginia's First Press Club Opens in Richmond in November." October 1953.

Wertheimer, Alfred. "Elvis '56; In the Beginning, an Intimate, Eyewitness Photo-journal." N.p., n.d.

Williams, Eda Carter. "General Foch, Marshal of France, Visits Richmond: November 23, 1921, a Day to Remember." *Richmond Literature and History Quarterly* 12 (Spring 1990).

————. "The Jefferson Hotel—A Recollection or How I Got My Richmond Friends." *Richmond Literature and History Quarterly* 8 (Winter 1985).

Williams, Michael Paul. "Jefferson to Remain Open, Official Says of Foreclosure." *Richmond Times Dispatch*, 1989.

Winstead, Joy. "Rotunda Club Memories Got Down to Bare Facts." *Richmond Times Dispatch*, May 4, 1986.

Wolf, Carol O'Connor. "The Re-Making of The Jefferson." *Style Weekly* March 11, 1986.

Books

Bak, Richard. *The Big Jump: Lindbergh and the Great Atlantic Air Race.* Hoboken, NJ: John Wiley & Sons, 2011.

Bearss, Sara B., ed. *Dictionary of Virginia Biography.* Richmond: Library of Virginia, 1998–2006.

Blake, Curtis Channing. *The Architecture of Carrere & Hastings.* N.p.: University Microfilms International, 1979.

Bryson, Bill. *At Home.* New York: Doubleday, 2010.

Caravati, Charles M. *Major James Dooley.* Richmond, VA: published for the Maymont Foundation, 1978.

Evans, Clemant A., ed. *Confederate Military History.* Atlanta, GA: Confederate Publishing Co., 1899.

Fox, James. *Five Sisters: The Langhornes of Virginia.* New York: Simon & Schuster, 2000.

Gibson, Langhorne, Jr. *The Gibson Girl: Portrait of a Southern Belle.* Richmond, VA: Commodore Press, 1997.

Kaplan, Justin. *When the Astors Owned New York.* New York: Viking, 2006.

Krick, Robert E.L., ed. *Staff Officers in Gray, A Biographical Register of the Staff Officers in the Army of Northern Virginia.* Chapel Hill: University of North Carolina Press, 2003.

Moore, Samuel J., Jr. *The Jefferson Hotel: A Southern Landmark.* Richmond, VA, 1940.

Morton, Richard L., et al. *The History of Virginia.* Chicago: American Historical Society, 1924.

Rousch, Elizabeth. *Getty*. Richmond, VA: William Byrd Press, 1964.

Salmon, Emily J., and Edward D.C. Campbell Jr., eds. *Hornbook of Virginia History*. Richmond: Virginia State Library, 1983.

Stewart, Colonel William H., ed. *History of Norfolk County, Virginia and Representatives Citizens*. Chicago: Biographical Publishing Company, 1902.

Tyler, Lyon G. *Encyclopedia of Biography*. Vol. 4. New York: Lewis Historical Publishing Co., 1915.

———. *Men of Mark in Virginia*. Richmond, VA: Men of Mark Publishing Co., 1936.

NEWSPAPERS

Alexandria [Viginia] *Gazette*, December 23, 1903; April 28, 1908.

Atlanta Constitution, July 15, 1902; May 13, 1915.

Baltimore Sun, May 25, 1908; December 22, 1904; February 14, 1901; December 19, 1924.

Carbondale [Illinois] *Free Press*, June 17, 1899.

Colorado Springs Gazette, April 28, 1967.

Daily News Record [Harrisonburg, Virginia], June 5, 1987.

Danville [Virginia] *Bee*, September 10, 1928.

Free Lance Star [Fredericksburg, Virginia], January 3, 1911; March 29, 1932; September 17, 1954; March 10, 1945.

Honolulu Evening Bulletin, January 25, 1905.

Janesville [Illinois] *Daily Gazette*, October 18, 1905.

Lima [Ohio] *Daily News*, September 24, 1907.

Lowell [Massachusetts] *Sun*, May 24, 1909.

Mansfield [Ohio] *News*, June 21, 1912.

Massillon [Ohio] *Item*, December 30, 1898.

Mathews Journal, February 22, 1912; May 22, 1912; August 22, 1912.

Middleton Daily Argus, September 19, 1896.

New York American, February 14, 1908.

New York Evening World, July 15, 1902; November 26, 1902; December 24, 1907; April 27, 1908.

New York Sun, April 30, 1895; December 22, 1903; November 14, 1906; February 23, 1908; May 28, 1908; May 30, 1908; June 11, 1909; May 29, 1910.

New York Times, April 19, 1899; December 28, 1900; December 21, 1902; September 28, 1904; May 5, 1908; July 15, 1917; May 20,

1923; November 19, 1925; September 30, 1934; December 20, 1934; December 12, 1921; April 3, 1926; July 19, 1924; June 17, 1926; October 25, 1947; June 9, 1968.

New York Tribune, November 24, 1895; September 11, 1896; July 17, 1901; July 21, 1901; July 8, 1902; July 15, 1902; July 23, 1902; August 21, 1902; December 23, 1902; November 15, 1903; September 4, 1904; September 28, 1904; December 14, 1907; March 28, 1908; July 26, 1908; September 16, 1908; September 9, 1909; December 31, 1910; November 11, 1912; October 1, 1913; April 22, 1915; April 27, 1916; December 18, 1920; February 12, 1922; March 9, 1922.

Pensacola Journal, October 31, 1908.

Petersburg [Virginia] *Daily Progress*, March 23, 1912; September 28, 1914.

Philadelphia Evening Ledger, August 12, 1915.

Philadelphia Inquirer, May 26, 1900.

Providence [Rhode Island] *News*, June 5, 1922.

Richmond Dispatch, January 13, 1893; February 21, 1893; March 9, 1894; September 11, 1894; October 28, 1894; March 7, 1895; October 26, 1895; November 27, 1895; November 28, 1895; December 24, 1895; February 2, 1896; February 18, 1896; March 29, 1896; March 31, 1896; April 16, 1896; June 30, 1896; August 2, 1896; October 30, 1896; February 9, 1897; February 13, 1897; March 28, 1897; April 8, 1897; April 18, 1897; June 6, 1897; September 1, 1897; October 3, 1897; November 3, 1897; November 7, 1897; January 30, 1898; March 20, 1898; May 12, 1898; May 15, 1898; May 29, 1898; June 5, 1898; June 9, 1898; June 22, 1898; July 17, 1898; September 4, 1895; October 22, 1898; October 14, 1900; May 17, 1899; January 4, 1900; January 10, 1900; January 11, 1900; January 22, 1900; January 20, 1900; January 28, 1900; January 31, 1900; February 7, 1900; February 18, 1900; February 23, 1900; March 6, 1900; March 14, 1900; April 30, 1900; April 19, 1900; May 1, 1900; May 6, 1900; May 24, 1900; May 31, 1900; June 19, 1900; June 20, 1900; July 7, 1900; September 1, 1900; October 10, 1900; November 9, 1900; November 16, 1900; November 21, 1900; November 25, 1900; November 27, 1900; December 1, 1900; December 12, 1900; December 21, 1902; January 1, 1901; January 24, 1901; January 27, 1901; February 5, 1901; February 6, 1901; February 14, 1901; February 15, 1901; February 17, 1901; February 21, 1901; February 22, 1901; March 2, 1901; March 6, 1901; March 7, 1901; March 14, 1901; March 16, 1901; March 18, 1901; March 20, 1901; March 24, 1901; March 27, 1901; December 24, 1901; January 1, 1902;

January 26, 1902; February 16, 1902; March 1, 1902; March 2, 1902; March 29, 1902; April 19, 1902; April 30, 1902; May 16, 1902; May 18, 1902; May 21, 1902; May 23, 1902; May 27, 1902; May 28, 1902; May 29, 1902; July 16, 1902; August 15, 1902; August 30, 1902; September 2, 1902; September 9, 1902; October 5, 1902; October 29, 1902; October 31, 1902; November 9, 1902; November 16, 1902; November 25, 1902; November 27, 1902; December 13, 1902; December 23, 1902.

Richmond News Leader, May 6, 1955; July 15, 1955; May 18, 1964; August 3, 1974; May 28, 1975; October 6, 1976; November 3, 1978; December 10, 1978; December 8, 1980; June 28, 1984; September 21, 1990.

Richmond Times, October 3, 1897; October 4, 1897; November 27, 1898; February 7, 1900; February 8, 1900; February 14, 1900; February 15, 1900; May 6, 1900; May 8, 1900; May 9, 1900; May 12, 1900; May 16, 1900; November 25, 1900; April 24, 1902; July 15, 1902.

Richmond Times Dispatch, February 10, 1903; February 15, 1903; February 20, 1903; February 21, 1903; March 31, 1903; April 5, 1903; April 7, 1903; April 8, 1903; April 12, 1903; April 26, 1903; May 9, 1903; May 14, 1903; May 15, 1903; June 4, 1903; June 16, 1903; July 7, 1903; August 2, 1903; August 20, 1903; September 3, 1903; September 9, 1903; September 11, 1903; September 20, 1903; October 18, 1903; October 20, 1903; October 21, 1903; October 22, 1903; October 24, 1903; November 24, 1903; November 29, 1903; December 16, 1903; December 23, 1903; December 24, 1903; December 30, 1903; January 23, 1904; March 1, 1904; March 16, 1904; March 17, 1904; March 30, 1904; April 1, 1904; April 6, 1904; April 19, 1904; June 1, 1904; July 5, 1904; August 11, 1904; August 21, 1904; October 10, 1904; November 12, 1904; December 17, 1904; January 4, 1905; January 25, 1905; March 16, 1905; March 18, 1905; March 19, 1905; April 2, 1905; April 20, 1905; April 27, 1905; May 24, 1905; May 25, 1905; June 6, 1905; June 30, 1905; July 4, 1905; July 22, 1905; August 6, 1905; August 9, 1905; August 11, 1905; August 13, 1905; August 18, 1905; August 25, 1905; September 23, 1905; October 8, 1905; October 18, 1905; October 30, 1905; November 2, 1905; January 1, 1906; January 27, 1906; March 31, 1906; April 23, 1906; May 2, 1906; July 10, 1906; August 2, 1906; August 12, 1906; February 15, 1907; February 27, 1907; January 7, 1908; January 9, 1908; January 31, 1908; January 27, 1908; February 2, 1908; February 5, 1908; February 6, 1908; February 24, 1908; February 26, 1908; March 3, 1908; March 4, 1908; March 6, 1908; March 7, 1908; March 23, 1908; March 24, 1908; March 25, 1908; April 7, 1908; April

13, 1908; April 18, 1908; April 21, 1908; April 27, 1908; April 28, 1908; April 29, 1908; May 1, 1908; May 10, 1908; May 16, 1908; May 20, 1908; May 22, 1908; May 23, 1908; May 24, 1908; May 26, 1908; June 21, 1908; July 1, 1908; August 5, 1908; August 15, 1908; September 10, 1908; September 12, 1908; September 17, 1908; September 28, 1908; October 5, 1908; October 8, 1908; October 9, 1908; October 17, 1908; October 20, 1908; October 23, 1908; October 28, 1908; November 14, 1908; November 19, 1908; November 21, 1908; November 22, 1908; December 29, 1908; January 14, 1909; January 16, 1909; February 15, 1909; March 11, 1909; March 27, 1909; April 1, 1909; April 3, 1909; April 9, 1909; April 16, 1909; April 17, 1909; April 19, 1909; April 28, 1909; April 30, 1909; June 4, 1909; June 12, 1909; August 30, 1909; September 13, 1909; September 22, 1909; September 23, 1909; October 3, 1909; October 11, 1909; October 12, 1909; November 10, 1909; November 16, 1909; November 29, 1909; December 2, 1909; January 14, 1910; January 27, 1910; February 2, 1910; February 7, 1910; March 9, 1910; May 10, 1910; May 11, 1910; June 14, 1910; June 28, 1910; July 12, 1910; August 2, 1910; September 26, 1910; October 17, 1910; October 18, 1910; November 1, 1910; November 22, 1910; December 1, 1910; January 5, 1911; March 5, 1911; March 26, 1911; May 14, 1911; May 16, 1911; June 11, 1911; June 25, 1911; June 27, 1911; June 28, 1911; January 9, 1913; January 26, 1913; April 9, 1913; August 22, 1913; January 14, 1914; March 27, 1915; February 19, 1919; November 8, 1929; June 7, 1934; August 20, 1935; March 16, 1936; June 7, 1940; February 25, 1941; January 12, 1943; February 16, 1943; March 10, 1944; March 11, 1944; March 12, 1944; March 13, 1944; March 15, 1944; March 16, 1944; March 18, 1944; March 27, 1944; April 14, 1944; August 22, 1944; October 25, 1944; November 11, 1944; February 17, 1945; February 26, 1945; March 5, 1945; March 6, 1945; July 18, 1945; July 23, 1945; February 19, 1946; April 3, 1946; April 16, 1949; May 15, 1949; August 29, 1949; March 22, 1950; August 26, 1951; December 7, 1951; September 20, 1953; February 4, 1954; February 6, 1954; April 25, 1954; October 11, 1954; October 13, 1954; March 13, 1955; April 6, 1956; July 4, 1956; May 7, 1957; September 27, 1957; January 28, 1958; April 11, 1958; September 18, 1959; May 18, 1960; April 19, 1961; September 29, 1961; January 2, 1963; January 3, 1963; October 13, 1964; October 17, 1964; November 8, 1966; November 26, 1966; November 27, 1966; September 23, 1968; January 3, 1969; April 2, 1969; April 8, 1969; March 24, 1970; August 30, 1970; January 24,

1971; May 12, 1971; September 17, 1972; February 23, 1973; February 24, 1973; September 25, 1973; June 20, 1974; March 26, 1975; May 6, 1975; July 27, 1976; November 11, 1976; January 26, 1977; March 13, 1980; May 22, 1980; August 16, 1980; December 4, 1980; September 10, 1983; November 13, 1983; March 31, 1984; July 4, 1991.

San Francisco Call, May 25, 1900; September 29, 1904; May 14, 1905; January 13, 1906.

Sarasota Herald Tribune, March 6, 1928; March 16, 1947.

Seattle Daily Times, August 20, 1911; July 17, 1916; December 10, 1916; January 5, 1928.

Spartanburg Herald Journal, September 22, 1946.

St. Paul Globe, June 2, 1901.

Syracuse Herald, Match 7, 1909.

Titusville [Pennsylvania] *Morning Herald*, November 1, 1899.

Trenton Evening Times, July 1, 1898; February 22, 1900; February 23, 1900; May 14, 1900; October 14, 1900; October 21, 1900; July 6, 1902; January 24, 1909; May 18, 1911; October 17, 1911; October 9, 1914; March 27, 1915; June 25, 1915; January 17, 1939; March 12, 1944; June 12, 1950.

Washington Herald, January 5, 1907; February 22, 1914.

Washington Post, September 29, 1904; October 16, 1904; September 24, 1905; October 6, 1905; October 7, 1905; October 20, 1906; May 5, 1908; September 23, 1909; November 28, 1909; December 12, 1909; November 24, 1910; November 27, 1910; January 8, 1911; January 30, 1911; February 5, 1911; February 19, 1911; September 5, 1911; February 10, 1918.

Washington Times, March 21, 1908; May 21, 1912.

OTHER SOURCES

Belvedere Hotel Records. University of Baltimore, Langsdale Library. Information about Esther Price courtesy of the Western Historical Manuscript Collection, Rolla, Missouri.

Calisch, Nicki. *Smoke in a Package: The Story of Major Lewis Ginter*. N.p., n.d.

Graham, John Paul. "Carrere and Hastings in Richmond, Virginia." Master's thesis, January 1988.

Information about Charles Consolvo courtesy of the Sargeant Memorial Collection, Norfolk Public Library.

Jefferson Hotel memorabilia and photos: Jefferson Hotel, George T. Ross, Mary Stuart Cruickshank, James Oliver Images, Sue Dayton, Fran Kizer, Jeanita Harris.

Peter M. Fry Scrapbook and Elinor Fry Scrapbook courtesy of Bettie Terrell Hobson.

Special Collections and Archives, James Branch Cabell Library, Virginia Commonwealth University Libraries:

Caperton, Helena Lefroy. "Laying of The Jefferson Hotel Corner Stone" and "Welcome."

Grace Arents letter and information about Mrs. Alfred Dieterich.

Sue Powell Williams's Scrapbooks. Courtesy of Susan Powell Williams.

Valentine Museum:

Polk Miller Scrapbooks.

Tobacco Ball Festival programs.

Valentine Auction Book.

Various receipts and invoices.

Virginia Acts and Joint Resolutions Passed by the General Assembly of the State of Virginia During the Session of 1899–1900.

Virginia Historical Society Collection:

Declaration of Convictions Adopted at the First Annual Convention of the Defenders of State Sovereignty and Individual Liberties.

Fred Anderson, "Born on the Fourth of July."

Fifth Annual Tour program.

George Wesley Rogers, ed. Officers of the Senate of Virginia: 1776–1956.

Harry Truman letter, September 2, 1940.

James, Isaac. "The Sun Do Move: The Story of the Life of John Jasper." Sermon, n.d.

Joseph Bryan Letter Book.

Ladies' Night Richmond Rotary Club song folder and program.

Lewis Ginter passport.

Richmond Literature and History Quarterly 6 (Summer 1983). Quote about recollection of Teddy Roosevelt's visit to Richmond.

Williams, Lewis C. Letter to the editor. Commonwealth Magazine (March 1951).

Worsham, Gibson. "The École des Beaux-Arts and Carrere and Hastings' Jefferson Hotel." Urban Scale Richmond. http://urbanscalerichmondvirginia.blogspot.com.

About the Author

Paul N. Herbert is the author of *God Knows All Your Names*, a collection of true stories of obscure events in American history, including an analysis of Abraham Lincoln's personal bank records, POWs held in the United States during World War II, the physician-spy of the American Revolution and the Radium Girls. He can be reached by e-mail at pnh9202@verizon.net.